SCM STUDYGUIDE TO BIBLICAL HERMENEUTICS

David A. Holgate
and
Rachel Starr

scm press

For our parents

British Library Cataloguing in Publication data

A catalogue record for this book is available
from the British Library.

0 334 04004 3
9780 334 04004 0

First published in 2006 by SCM Press
9–17 St Alban's Place,
London N1 0NX

www.scm-canterburypress.co.uk

SCM Press is a division of
SCM-Canterbury Press Ltd

Typeset by Regent Typesetting
Printed and bound in Great Britain by
Creative Print and Design, Wales

Contents

Acknowledgements

We have been preparing this book for a number of years, working with teaching colleagues and students of the Southern Theological Education and Training Scheme. Though the approach presented here is our own, we do wish to thank all those who have helped us develop it. Working together on this project has reminded us that biblical interpretation is a collaborative activity. We hope that you will find opportunities to interact with others each time you seek to work out what the Bible says to you today.

Introduction

Purpose

This book offers a framework for interpreting the Bible. It goes beyond showing you how to do exegesis and enables you to relate the Bible to your experience of everyday life. While we have tried to provide a clear approach to biblical interpretation, we do not intend to be prescriptive. We offer this Studyguide to you as a practical tool to help you to develop good interpretative strategies of your own. There should come a time when you feel confident enough to be able to set this book aside. By then, we hope that you will have proved to yourself that, while there is no single, agreed method for interpreting the Bible, there is a great deal of agreement on the resources that need to be used by responsible interpreters.

Practicalities

You can use this Studyguide in a number of ways. Initially, you may find it helpful just to review the Contents page and the Summary at the back. As you need to learn more about each of the steps in this process, we hope that you will read through each chapter more fully. Please enter into dialogue with the book.

Where you disagree with something, explain to yourself why you do so and offer a better alternative. This will help you develop an interpretative strategy of your own. As you use this Studyguide to develop your skills, we hope that the 'Try it out' boxes will offer you practical help with the passage you are working on.

David Holgate and Rachel Starr

1

Where Do We Want to Go?

Using this book

This Studyguide is designed to help you become a better Bible reader and interpreter. It offers you an integrated way of using a whole range of critical methods to enable you to interpret biblical passages for yourself. Unlike some biblical guides, it does not suggest it is possible to arrive at one final correct interpretation of any passage. Rather, the process outlined here is designed to guide you towards making responsible provisional interpretations of your own, ones that you can develop in the light of new information, about yourself, the world and the Bible. The Studyguide is intended to be used as a complete process, rather than as a reference book or dictionary.

Alongside this book, you may find it helpful to have access to a dictionary of biblical interpretation, to look up short descriptions of the key words and concepts discussed here. One book often referred to here is the *Handbook of Biblical Interpretation* (third edition, 2001) by the father and son team of R. N. and R. K. Soulen. *To Each Its Own Meaning*, edited by S. L. McKenzie and S. R. Haynes (revised and expanded third edition, 1999) offers fuller critical evaluations of many of the approaches covered here, though not all. A growing number of websites offer reliable online reference information too. For example, the site: http://sim74.kenrickparish.com/cbi/ provides a useful general outline of biblical interpretation from a Roman Catholic perspective.

Identifying our reason for reading the Bible

Each time we turn to the Bible, we do so with a particular purpose, for example, to refer to a passage as background reading for a literature course, or to learn more about Christian or Jewish beliefs. But we also have a wider reason that motivates our use of the Bible, for example, we may read it because we regard it as a sacred book, a great literary work, or a useful historical source. Or we may have some other reason.

> **Try it out**
>
> Jot down a few thoughts on how you see the Bible and then try to state your overall reason for reading the Bible.

There are many different reasons for studying the Bible, all with different goals and outcomes. This Studyguide regards the Bible as a text of great importance for the academy, for faith communities and for the wider world. For all of these contexts, it promotes a method of reading the Bible that is an ongoing quest for life-affirming interpretations of the text. All readers of the Bible need to recognize that the Bible witnesses to the faith of the communities from which it arose, even though clearly not all readers will share this faith. While the authors write from a Christian perspective and believe that the Bible informs, enriches and directs their interaction with God, the method outlined here recognizes that other people read the Bible with other eyes and commitments and that such readings are also valid.

Identifying our reason for reading a passage

However we regard the Bible at the moment, it is worth answering two quite practical questions before we open it.

- What do we want from the Bible, for ourselves and for others?
- And therefore which passage(s) are we going to read?

The Bible is a collection of books most of which have a long history of development and all of which have a long history of interpretation and influence. This means that the Bible is a complex text which can be difficult to handle. As readers, our own context and identity change over time and this also affects our reading of the Bible. To avoid getting lost in a sea of questions, each time we read the Bible, we should clarify our purpose in doing so to help focus our study.

Biblical interpretation is a skill which can only be developed through practice. Throughout this book we invite you to try things out for yourself, using the 'Try it out' boxes to develop your skills in different areas. Please use this 'Try it out' box now before reading further.

> ### Try it out
>
> To explore your changing relationship with the Bible, turn to the well-known story of David's combat with Goliath in 1 Samuel 17 and read it. Be alert to how you relate to this text here and now. What questions do you have for this text today, and what questions does it have for you?

The story of David and Goliath is often included in illustrated collections of Bible stories for children, and when the title is mentioned we may find that our first memories are of such a version. There are many good things about reading the Bible as a child that we should maintain as adults: children read playfully and imaginatively. But, we may not have been told the whole story as children. Reading the David and Goliath story as adults may raise many new questions for us:

Historical questions:
- When did this happen?
- Why were the Israelites and the Philistines at loggerheads?

Geographical questions:
- Where did this encounter take place?
- Where are Socoh and Azekah?

Cultural questions:
- Was David following normal military practice by cutting off the head of his dead enemy?
- Why did the Israelites slaughter their defeated enemies as they fled?

A question about how this text might relate to Israel/Palestine today:
- Has this region always been particularly prone to conflict between groups?

A question about the continuity of the 1 Samuel narrative:
- If David is presented as a skilled musician and warrior in 1 Samuel 16, why is he described in verse 42 as 'only a youth'?

A more modern psychological question:
- Wasn't the young David traumatized by having to carry his enemy's head with him, e.g. holding it 'in his hand' when he went into King Saul's presence (v. 57)? How might this have affected the course of his later life?

By reading this passage afresh, we notice the strangeness of even the most familiar Bible story. Thinking back on our prior knowledge of the story of David and Goliath we may notice how incompletely we recalled it, perhaps because it was told to us very selectively as children. Equally, we may have once heard a sermon on the passage which held up David as an example of faith. Yet, reading it now against, for example, reports of death and dismemberment in the Middle East, such an interpretation may strike us as inadequate because it fails to recognize the violence in the text and relate this to the violence in the present.

If we try to insist that this account is not really about warfare, but rather deeper spiritual or theological matters, then we only need to look back to the last ten verses of 1 Samuel 16.14–23. Verse 14 makes an awkward start, for it describes the Lord sending an evil spirit to torment (another translation says, 'terrorize') King Saul. In case we have missed this shocking statement, the next verse describes the king's servants as saying to him, 'See now, an evil spirit from God is tormenting you.' We then find ourselves with a theological problem and have to ask what sort of God 1 Samuel 16–17 presents.

The above example shows how quickly our Bible reading can raise interpretative problems for us. To help us sort out which of these issues we are to work on and which to set aside for the present we look again at our overall purpose in reading the Bible and our present goal in reading this passage. We cannot and do not need to tackle every sort of question at once.

> ## Try it out
>
> Think of your goal and your immediate purpose in reading whatever biblical text you are currently studying. These will normally be determined by some everyday need that provides you with a focus for study.

There are many reasons why we engage in biblical interpretation:

- A crisis may have erupted locally, nationally or internationally and people are asking big questions about the nature of life and human relationships. We turn to the Bible for moral guidance or support.
- We are involved in formal teaching, and have to provide a considered answer to a matter of interpretation; for example, what do different parts of the Bible teach about human sexuality?
- We are studying some aspect of the history of western culture and have come across a biblical reference that we need to understand.
- We are facing a personal crisis or moment of decision and are desperate for some form of outside input to help us decide, and hope that the Bible can offer some guidance.
- We have recently seen a play or film, read something, listened to a song, heard a comment, or visited a building and been struck by the way a biblical reference or theme is reflected there.
- We are involved in church leadership and are expected to preach on a particular Bible passage that we don't know very well, or at all!

We try to interpret the Bible for all sorts of reasons but the questions with which we turn to the Bible are not always the ones it answers. The text often leads us in a different direction, provoking other questions to the ones we began with. Because of the propensity of the Bible to send us off somewhere else, it is necessary for us to plot where we are now and where we hope to get to at the outset, a bit like a sailor setting off on a course with many potential hazards and diversions. If we know where we have started from and where we are aiming for, we can check our progress along the way. In biblical interpretation this does not, or should not, guarantee that we will arrive at our intended destination; certainly not in the sense of arriving at the conclusions that we expected at the outset. But it will help us to place limits upon our enquiry and ask the right questions of the text. If we find ourselves blown off course by the force of the passage, at least we will know this and be able to account for it. Perhaps the original questions we began with have not been answered by the text but we have been moved to seek answers to other questions that now seem more important.

Provisional and responsible interpretation

As we noted at the start of this chapter, this Studyguide suggests that it is not possible to arrive at a final, definitive interpretation of any biblical passage, but that it is possible to work towards arriving at a responsible interpretation of a passage for a particular purpose at a particular time. This is a vantage point in an ongoing journey towards deeper understanding of the Bible, of ourselves, and of the world we inhabit.

Our aim should be to offer our provisional interpretation with self-awareness, making evident to ourselves and our hearers or readers that we know what is driving us, and understand that our circumstances and beliefs limit just how widely our interpretation is applicable for others. The perspectives and tools employed here require us to respect both the integrity of the biblical text and of our own lives. Our work of interpretation needs to be done with integrity and honesty, resisting temptations to short-change ourselves or others with simplistic or trite answers. We should try to bring our deepest and truest questions and convictions to our conversation with the Bible, and seek the best answers we can arrive at.

Try it out

The Lord's Prayer is one of the most well-known passages in the Bible, so it is likely that you will already know something about it. Perhaps you know it by heart. If so, recite it to yourself. What do you think it is about?

Now read Matthew 6.9–13 carefully and attentively. In what way does this reading confirm or question your prior understanding of this passage? How does your current life situation affect your reading and give you different insights to previous readings? How might you test out whether your reading is a responsible one?

2

Past Experience and Present Expectations

The Bible's influence

In Chapter 1, we identified our starting point and began to consider our overall reason for studying the Bible as well as the particular task in hand. The next step in the process is to clarify our relationship with the Bible, so this chapter considers how our previous collective and individual experience of the Bible affects our interpretative task.

The stories and ideas recorded within the Bible have shaped our reality in many ways. Throughout history, people have used the Bible to control and oppress others as well as to encourage and support them and we must take account of this mixed legacy in our interpretations.

The stories of the Bible are powerful because they are a testimony to people's lives – of travellers on the move as well as settled communities. The Bible speaks of human reality and thus of our own reality. It is, moreover, a story of particular encounters with God. It is a story of mystery and holiness – the holy things of liturgy and ritual but also of human relationships, of loss and joy.

The Bible's status also comes from its value as a holy object. Witnesses in an English court of law usually take an oath on the Bible or another holy book to tell the truth. The power invested in the Bible is demonstrated in other ways around the world, e.g. Brazilian Christians might bury a Bible in the foundations of their new house for good luck (Schroer 2003, p. 8).

The power of the Bible is, to an extent, determined by how we respond to it. If we choose to disregard the Bible it has no immediate power over us. However, our historic relationship with the Bible is such that its influence will be felt upon us, whether or not we regard it as a sacred book. So great is this cultural influence that many people within the West, even those who would not identify themselves as part of the church, have been taught and, to an extent, accepted unquestioningly, biblical stories and teaching such as the Ten Commandments. Such trust is illustrated by this traditional Sunday school verse:

Jesus loves me this I know, because the Bible tells me so.
I love Jesus yes I do, because the Bible tells me to.

Even in today's multi-faith Britain, young children grow up hearing Bible stories from their parents, teachers or even the television. Indeed, it is hard to imagine how those of us who were raised in a nominally Christian context can ever read the Bible without some prior knowledge of its stories, characters and teachings. Of course, this makes it harder to discern what a text might have to say to us in the present moment. In some ways we have to 'unlearn' what we have been told about the Bible in order to read it afresh.

From childhood, we may recall exciting heroes and vivid stories, related as part myth, part moral instruction. As adults, we need to move to a more (or differently) critical understanding of these stories and characters. We have already reflected on how stories such as that of David and Goliath are presented to children in a sanitized fashion that glamorizes the violent reality of the event. The process of re-evaluating childhood stories is a difficult one, and the image we build up as children about a biblical event may be impossible to leave behind completely. Moreover, there may well be elements of insight and truth in these early interpretations that will serve us well throughout our lives. What we need to ensure is that we are free to reassess and revaluate biblical passages that are deeply embedded in our memories in order that they can remain relevant to us in our adult lives.

Try it out

What are some of your earliest beliefs about the Bible? When did you first encounter the Bible, in childhood or later in life? Make a list of images or phrases that highlight how you were introduced to it. How has your understanding of the Bible changed during your life?

In the United Kingdom Census of 2001, 72 per cent of respondents described themselves as Christian. Despite secularization, it would seem that there are still many in Britain and Northern Ireland who like to see themselves as people who respect the Bible, even if they prefer to keep it at a respectable distance! Yet there is no doubt that churchgoing is a declining activity in the UK, and even regular churchgoers often have significant gaps in their biblical knowledge.

In contrast to the somewhat superficial knowledge of the Bible encountered within nominally Christian contexts, many Jewish and Muslim communities have a deeper collective knowledge of their holy books. Here there is often a living knowledge of Scripture that comes from a regular encounter with text during times of prayer, as well as knowledge of the original language (Hebrew, Aramaic or Arabic). In a synagogue, for example, the Torah is first read in Hebrew followed by a translation into the local language or vernacular.

Try it out

Ask a person of a faith other than your own, or the one you are most familiar with, about their knowledge and understanding of their sacred texts.

The extent of our knowledge about the Bible and how we received that knowledge (during childhood, as an adult, as a devout Christian or Jew, as an academic student) will affect what we expect to encounter when we read and interpret it.

The Bible in society

The Bible has been instrumental in constructing, shaping and even destroying social structures. This diversity is not simply the result of interpretative differences since the Bible itself expresses a range of social views, with some traditions advocating social conservatism and others, social radicalism. This is particularly apparent in the Hebrew Bible's variant attitudes towards the monarchy, e.g. 1 Samuel 7–15 includes two perspectives: that monarchy is God's will and that it is an act of infidelity. No clear answer to the dispute over the institute of kingship is given (Brueggemann 1997b, p. 72).

Try it out

How would you assess the social and political impact of the Bible in the countries you have lived in? One example you could consider is the British legal system. What kind of social and political impact do you think the Bible should have?

Over the centuries, numerous political and religious rulers have seen in the Bible support for their own agenda. Some have used it to maintain the status quo, to preserve 'Christian culture', or to justify 'one nation under God'. Others have read the Bible as a mandate for invasion and used it as an instrument of colonial intrusion. In response, African-American scholar Renita Weems notes:

> The Bible cannot go unchallenged in so far as the role it has played in legitimating the dehumanization of people of African ancestry in general and the sexual exploitation of women of African ancestry in particular. It cannot be understood as some universal, transcendent, timeless force to which world readers – in the name of being pious and faithful followers – must meekly submit. It must be understood as a politically and socially drenched text invested in ordering relations between people, legitimating some viewpoints and delegitimizing other viewpoints. (Weems 2003, p. 24)

While cautious of its negative impact, liberationist movements have also understood the Bible to be a text for freedom. Elsa Tamez, who teaches at a seminary in Costa Rica, describes how through the liberation theology movement, 'The Bible took on new meaning ... [It] became the simple text that speaks of a loving, just, liberating God who accompanied the poor in their suffering and their struggle through human history' (Tamez 1995, p. 48).

In apartheid South Africa, both sides used the Bible to justify their actions. Although the Dutch Reformed Church believed they had biblical support for racial discrimination, Desmond Tutu warned the apartheid regime:

> ... the Bible is the most revolutionary, the most radical book there is. If a book had to be banned by those who rule unjustly and as tyrants, then it ought to have been the Bible. Whites brought us the Bible and we are taking it seriously. (Tutu 1994, p. 72)

Let us look more closely at three examples of the divergent roles the Bible can play in the creation of social and political structures.

Fairfield Moravian Settlement

In the early 1700s, the Moravian community at Herrnhut, Germany drew up a document called *The Brotherly Agreement*. Drawing closely from the Bible, this text, known today as *The Moravian Covenant for Christian Living* forms the basis for Moravian community life. The following extract illustrates this method of forming social relationships on biblical teachings:

> 15. We will endeavor to settle our differences with others in a Christian manner (Galatians 6.1), amicably, and with meditation, and, if at all possible, avoid resort to a court of law (Matthew 18.15–17).
> Taken from: www.everydaycounselor.com/archives/sh/covenant.htm

Moravians established a number of communities in Britain. The Fairfield Moravian Settlement on the outskirts of Manchester was founded in 1785.

It was self-sufficient with its own church, schools, bakery and farm. Today the community continues to support mission and social welfare projects, including sheltered housing. (Summarized from: www.billnkaz.demon.co.uk/moravian.htm)

The website of the Moravian Church in the UK is: www.moravian.org.uk

The Bible and the conquest of Latin America

For our second example we look at how the Bible has on occasions been used to justify violence against non-Christian nations. The conquest of Latin America from the fifteenth century was a religious as well as a political event. The explorer Christopher Columbus and his royal backers in the Spanish court argued that the invasion and colonization was primarily motivated by evangelistic desire. But for the indigenous people it was a 'mad time' as this testimony from the Mayan book of the Linajes recalls:

> It was only because of the mad time, the mad priests, that sadness came among us, that Christianity came among us, for the great Christians came here with the true God; but that was the beginning of our distress ...
> the beginning of being stripped for everything,
> the beginning of slavery for debts.
> It was the beginning of the work of the Spaniards and the priests ...
> (Cited in Richard 1990, p. 60)

The Bible constituted a central part of the Spaniards' justification and the conquistadors even used the invasion of Canaan as a biblical model from which to validate their actions. Almost five hundred years later, indigenous people continued to protest against this abuse of the Bible. When Pope John Paul II visited Peru, indigenous groups sent him the following note:

> John Paul II, we, Andean and American Indians, have decided to take advantage of your visit to return to you your Bible, since in five centuries it has not given us love, peace or justice.
> Please take back your Bible and give it back to our oppressors, because

they need moral teaching more that we do. Ever since the arrival of Christopher Columbus a culture, language, religion and values which belong to Europe have been imposed on Latin America by force.

The Bible came to us as part of the imposed colonial transformation. It was the ideological weapon of this colonialist assault. The Spanish word which attacked and murdered the bodies of Indians by day and night became the cross which attacked the Indian soul. (Cited in Richard 1990, pp. 64–5)

The Gospel of Solentiname

Our final example is of liberative biblical interpretation. *The Gospel of Solentiname* is the title of a collection of transcripts of a Nicaraguan Bible study group that met weekly to discuss the Bible and their own situation. Led by the poet and priest, Ernesto Cardenal, the group was eventually disbanded by the conservative Nicaraguan government. For this group, and many others in Latin America and elsewhere, the Bible was transformed from an alien text into a story of hope and freedom.

Listen to the group discussing the anointing at Bethany: They struggle with Jesus words, 'the poor you will always have among you' (Matt. 26.11; Mark 14.7). Their discomfort is based on their experience of the reactionary ruling classes who used this phrase to justify continued inequalities. Through discussion, they try to reinterpret the phrase. Cardenal encourages the group to read the text carefully for themselves rather than relying on received interpretations. He suggests that Jesus means the poor will always be with the disciples, or his followers. Jesus' response could then be understood as a command to the church to locate itself with the poor, and to be the poor (Cardenal 1982, pp. 92–101).

In this section we have considered the persuasive force of the Bible over individuals, religious communities and even nations. This history of interpretation should caution us against using the Bible destructively. It is important that we are able to assess the role the Bible has played in the past and where necessary, be willing to challenge our relationship with it so that we can develop a more responsible and life-affirming interpretative method, for ourselves and for others.

Cultural interpretations of the Bible

For two thousand years, the Bible has influenced culture and art in many areas of the world. Indeed, religious material was the dominant subject of most art forms for many centuries. Beautiful paintings and sculptures in churches, public buildings and private homes represented the devotion of benefactors, artists and worshippers. These portrayals of biblical stories were also an invaluable teaching resource in illiterate communities.

Many classic paintings and works of literature are interpretations of a portion of the Bible. Our reading of the Bible is influenced by these portrayals in turn, for example, Leonardo da Vinci's *The Last Supper* has shaped western Christians' interpretation of this event for hundreds of years.

In his book, *The Return of the Prodigal Son*, Henri Nouwen recounts the deep impact of Rembrandt's painting of this parable on his spiritual journey. He spent many hours reflecting on the different characters in the painting and discovered how each one illuminated some aspect of his own story:

> When ... I went to Saint Petersburg to see Rembrandt's *The Return of the Prodigal Son*, I had little idea how much I would have to live what I then saw. I stand with awe at the place where Rembrandt brought me. He led me from the kneeling, dishevelled young son to the standing, bent-over old father, from the place of being blessed to the place of blessing. (Nouwen 1994, p. 139)

The painting, based on Luke 15.11–32, can be seen online at The Hermitage, St Petersburg: www.hermitagemuseum.org

Nouwen's testimony illuminates how artistic interpretations of the Bible can help us explore the written text in greater depth and complexity. Paintings, plays and poems may reveal connections between ourselves and a Bible passage that may not emerge from simply reading the text.

Try it out

Use an internet image search engine (or visit a local church or an art gallery) to see paintings of a biblical character or passages. Spend time reflecting on one or two classical or modern representations of the biblical figure or event. What do you think is the motivation of the artist? How do they retell the event? What new insights do they offer you about this passage?

Classical western literature is often in intentional dialogue with the Bible. There are hundreds of allusions to the Bible in the works of Shakespeare. Steven Marx's *Shakespeare and the Bible* (2000) explores how the playwright used the Bible to develop his narrative and characters. Marx compares, for example, the book of Job with *King Lear* and looks at the impact of Matthew's Gospel on *Measure for Measure*, in which characters reference (and occasionally misinterpret) the Gospel's teachings. One further example would be John Steinbeck's *East of Eden,* which explores the Genesis narrative, particularly the relationship between Cain and Abel (Genesis 4).

Literary versions of biblical stories have also influenced scholarly interpretation of texts. Thomas Mann's epic novel *Joseph and his Brothers* (published 1933–46) interpreted the story of Genesis for his context. Begun in Nazi Germany, it was completed in the USA following Mann's exile. As a novelist, Mann argued for the literary coherence of Genesis and his understanding of the story of Tamar and Judah (Genesis 38) as an integral part of the whole narrative, rather than a loosely related fragment, influenced later interpretations of Genesis.

The Bible itself has been studied as literature as well as a devotional text. In 1998, Canongate published individual books of the Bible marketing them as literary works, with introductions by writers, artists and politicians (www. canongate.net). For example, Bono from the band U2 wrote the introduction to the Psalms. Another singer, Nick Cave, in his introduction to Mark commented:

The Christ that emerges from *Mark*, tramping through the haphazard events of His life, had a ringing intensity about Him that I could not resist.

Christ spoke to me through His isolation, throughout the burden of His death, through His rage at the mundane, through His sorrow. (Cave 1998)

As story, rather than sacred text, Mark's Gospel was able to speak to Cave with a freshness and directness that he had not previously noticed. In Chapter 6, we will return to the method of reading the Bible as a story and our role as storytellers in this process.

Each generation retells the ancient biblical stories in new and different ways. The style, structure, language and meaning of a text can all be re-evaluated through new methods of retelling.

Try it out

Visit the Ship-of-Fools website where you can view several Bible verses rephrased in 'text' form: www.ship-of-fools.com/Features/0802/txt_comp.html

How do these paraphrases compare to the translation of the same passages in your version of the Bible? What aspects are highlighted in the text versions, and what response is required?

Contemporary culture is crammed with scriptural references, be it the Bible-quoting ex-con in *21 Grams* (2004); the sampling of spirituals in club music such as Moby's *Natural Blues* (1999); or Mark Wallinger's sculpture, *Ecce Homo* (1999) which, for a while, occupied the fourth plinth in Trafalgar Square.

Three useful websites for further research into the use of the Bible in film, music and literature today are:

www.textweek.com Textweek includes links to visual images of different biblical passages as well as summaries of films that refer to the Bible or biblical themes.

www.hollywoodjesus.com Hollywood Jesus includes reviews and reflections on films, television programmes and other media.

www.damaris.org Damaris offers study material on films, music and books but you have to subscribe to access this material.

In Chapter 3, we will explore in more detail how biblical texts have been interpreted over the centuries via research into impact history. For now, let us look at one example of pop culture's dialogue with Scripture taken from hip hop which, due to its gospel, soul and reggae influences, is often steeped in biblical language. Hip hop also attempts to create an alternative space in which to speak truths, and in this way parallels the reality transforming biblical texts.

Lauryn Hill's 1998 solo album *The Miseducation of Lauryn Hill* was her much-anticipated debut following previous releases with The Fugees. Robert Beckford comments:

> *The Miseducation of Lauryn Hill* ... utilizes biblical and theological themes such as judgment, salvation and justice ... For example in 'Final Hour', Hill weaves together biblical imagery with African American history, personal redemption and success, linking Moses and Aaron with Black resistance in America. (Beckford 2001, p. 102)

In the track, 'Final Hour', Hill raps more widely about God's justice, citing Psalm 73 as a text that strengthens her faith. Beckford notes that, 'central to this song is the belief that while material gain and position (money and power) are accessible, what is most important is God's judgement. Therefore it is essential that rappers "keep their eyes on the final hour"' (Beckford 2001, p. 124). Psalm 73 begins with the psalmist's questioning of God's justice since the wicked appear to prosper but goes on to reaffirm faith in God's final judgement. Meditation and prayer help the psalmist gain perspective, 'But when I thought how to understand this, it seemed to me a wearisome task, until I went into the sanctuary of God; then I perceived their end' (Psalm 73.16–17).

Hill's interpretation of Psalm 73 articulates the survival ethic of the African-American community: God is intent on preserving the community and ultimately, there will be just rewards for the faithful. But does 'Final

Hour' require white readers to reinterpret this psalm? The song brings into focus the contemporary identity of the wicked as well as the oppressed. If God is faithful to those who suffer from racism, then those who persist in upholding racist structures might not be 'always at ease' (Psalm 73.12).

Observing how the Bible is interpreted in everyday conversation and culture, offers us fresh ways of looking at Scripture. Such interpretations can reveal the impact a passage has had on a particular community and thus local interpreters sometimes function as guardians of a community's understandings of a text. Popular interpretations may sometimes be judged as misinterpretations, but they can still provoke new insight, revealing nuances and angles as yet hidden to academic readers.

The Sri Lankan-born, Birmingham-based scholar R. S. Sugirtharajah recently tracked biblical references in the British media. He notes the humorous irreverence of many ironic references as well as the continued cultural force of biblical quotes and allusions. Sugirtharajah describes much of the media's use of the Bible as simply 'looking for something that fits' (Sugirtharajah 2003, p. 78). However, he also notes the tremendous power that appeal to the Bible can have – both as a source of great comfort and as a means of oppression. Sugirtharajah describes much popular usage of Scripture as 'poaching' or taking what is needed from the whole narrative as and when necessary. Although alert to the dangers of this free-form, open-ended appropriation of the Bible, Sugirtharajah suggests it offers ordinary folk the opportunity to encounter Scripture on their own terms, without having its meaning restricted by academics (Sugirtharajah 2003, pp. 82–4).

Try it out

Do some informal research of your own – noting down any biblical references or allusions you encounter in the media, music, art and conversation during one day. Do these popular interpretations strengthen or change your existing understanding of the text referred to? Would you dispute any aspect of the popular interpretation, and on what grounds? Do you agree with Sugirtharajah's assessment of many popular references as 'poaching'?

The unfamiliar world of the Bible

We have begun to explore the many everyday situations in which we en-counter the Bible. Although each encounter may provide a different inter-pretation, there is a danger of becoming overly familiar with a text that we encounter many times, either culturally or as part of corporate worship or devotions. Texts such as Psalm 23, for example, may have lost their impact through frequent and uncritical use. Ronald Allen, who teaches preaching in Indianapolis, USA remarks, 'In exegesis, as in life, expectation plays an important role in fulfilment. What we expect is usually what we find' (Allen 1984, p. 22). If we believe the Bible to be a friendly, uncritical voice, then that is how we are likely to hear it.

Yet, the events, assumptions and locations of the Bible are actually un-familiar to most modern readers. No matter how familiar some passages may seem, the worlds of the Bible are very different to today's world. Allen warns against the cosy relationship American civil society has developed with the Bible:

> North American culture has co-opted the Bible as a source of blessing on our values, economic and political system, and life-style ... we have tended to regard the Bible as a word of confirmation of our way of life. In the United States it is easy to think of God as middle-class and the Bible as a kind of handbook for better family relationships. (Allen 1987, p. 23)

In the UK, this common cultural ease with the Bible is fast disintegrating as church attendance falls sharply, schools become more multifaith and global-ization offers new ways of understanding the world. However, the 'God is an Englishman' mentality prevails to a certain extent, with many English people still vaguely believing that the Christian God is located with them, can be understood through their cultural systems, and fully affirms their way of life.

In contrast, biblical scholars from Asia and Africa have become more in-sistent that we recognize the Bible did not originate in a western cultural context. For example, the South African-based translator Gosnell Yorke argues that the African context of various biblical events and communities has been hidden in Bible translations. He notes how in Genesis 2.10–14, translators have been reticent to identify Cush with modern-day Ethiopia and the Sudan, thus 'de-Africanizing' the text and denying the possibility that Eden was partially located in Africa (Yorke 2004, pp. 159–61).

R. S. Sugirtharajah has also written against the tendency to westernize the Bible, despite its eastern origins and influences. He highlights, for example, the comparative work done between Buddhist ideas and Christian texts such as John's Gospel, that may indicate shared patterns of thought and expression. He also observes the European focus on Paul's mission in Europe rather than Philip's earlier evangelism of the Ethiopian eunuch (Acts 8), and the impact this focus had on western missionary activity during colonialism (Sugirtharajah 2003, pp. 96–113). In response, one of the questions we should attend to as readers is how an interpretation of a biblical passage enables us to hear the Asian and African contexts and influences present within the text.

As well as the cultural differences between the modern western world and the worlds of the Bible, readers also have to contend with the revelatory claims of the text. If the Bible is regarded as a divine or sacred work, this will create distance between the text and the reader. Some interpreters suggest the Bible should be read with a sense of awe to allow its distinctive voice to be heard. In the 1930s, the Swiss theologian, Karl Barth sought to challenge the complacency of his fellow Christians. Against a background of a church co-opted by Nazism, he proclaimed the radically different word of God that challenges the presumption that we can meet or know God through human culture. Barth's work highlighted the strange, otherworldly nature of the Bible, which cuts across all rational human attempts at knowledge or justification. For Barth, the Bible reveals the awesome word of God to us that has the power to transform everything about us. 'Barth dared to assert the normative claim of the gospel defiantly against the landscape. What is normative is odd and peculiar, distinctive and scandalous, and can never be accommodated to the landscape of cultural ideology' (Brueggemann 1997b, p. 20).

Barth's work reminds us of the importance of allowing the Bible to speak on its own terms. As readers, we need to gain distance from the text so that we can come to the text anew, willing to be surprised. There is a creative tension that results from exploring the meaning of the Bible through cultural expression and human discourse while retaining a sense of the ultimately unknowable nature of God's word that can be encountered through the Bible.

The authority of the Bible

Jews and Christians believe the Bible to be a work of both divine and human origin, although they differ in their understanding of the balance between the two. Questions about how the Bible can be understood to be inspired by God are closely tied to understandings of the authority of the Bible. Put simply, those who believe that the words of the Bible are directly inspired by God, and who believe God is creator and judge of humans, are obliged to view the Bible as the absolute source of authority.

The Enlightenment encouraged scholars to find logical, provable sources of authority. In biblical studies it lead to a development of historical-critical methods concerned with discovering historical facts and extracting universal moral truths from the particularities of the biblical narrative. Parts of the Bible were thus awarded factual and moral authority.

Others approached the authority of the Bible quite differently. Rather than matching biblical teaching with contemporary scientific or historical theories, these Christians believed the authority of the Bible did not depend on rational argument but on its divine source alone. The biblical fundamentalism that emerged among North American Protestants in the early nineteenth century stringently defended the inerrancy of the Bible in response to the historical-critical movement. It taught the literal truth of the Bible and its wholly divine origins. But biblical fundamentalism has been widely criticized by scholars and church leaders. An official document of the Vatican published in 1993 denounced fundamentalism as 'a reading of the Bible which rejects all questionings and any kind of critical research' and further noted, 'The basic problem with fundamentalist interpretation of this kind is that, refusing to take into account the historical character of biblical revelation, it makes itself incapable of accepting the full truth of the incarnation itself' (The Pontifical Biblical Commission (1993) cited in Houlden 1995, p. 44). The Vatican argued that a fundamentalist approach to the Bible failed to acknowledge the Christian belief that God works with humans and entrusts the historical church with God's mission.

Nevertheless, fundamentalist approaches continue to hold their ground among some Christians. John Stackhouse, an evangelical scholar, observes how evangelicals see a direct relationship between matters of faith and the biblical teaching: 'we believe X because the Bible teaches it *right here*' (Stackhouse 2004, p. 187, Stackhouse's italics). Conservative evangelicals argue this direct application of biblical teaching is a sign of the central place of Bible in their faith. Such proof-texting (citing one or several biblical verses to support a point) often occurs in ethical debates, for example, protestors outside abortion clinics holding placards quoting biblical verses such as, 'For you created my inmost being; you knit me together in my mother's womb. I praise you because I am fearfully and wonderfully made' (Psalm 139.13–14). There are further examples of proof-texting at: http://bible.com/answers/answers.html

There are several problems with proof-texting as a responsible method of biblical application. The verse is isolated from its context within the wider narrative as well as its social context. Proof-texting suggests that a statement or example can be lifted from the page and applied directly to any situation in an ahistorical manner. Yet relying on isolated teaching in this way invests fragments of Scripture with exaggerated importance, independent of the wider story of faith.

While fundamentalism was a response to the historical critical method, as readers of the Bible today we also have to respond to postmodernism's rejection of all claims of authority as methods of control. Postmodernism expects us to take responsibility for the meaning of the text, denying the existence of any commonly agreed meaning.

Try it out

Which of these statements best describes your current view about the Bible?

- The Bible is the inspired word of God.
- The Bible is a human document inspired by the Holy Spirit but written by humans and it is possible that some of the divine message was corrupted in the process.

- The Bible is a record of various communities' shared history, communal identity and witness to God.
- The Bible is the word of God only when we enable it to be so by listening to God's word spoken to us through the text.
- The Bible is a collection of ancient writings irrelevant to today's society.

Robert Gnuse's *The Authority of the Bible: Theories of Inspiration, Revelation and the Canon of Scripture* explores the range of theological positions held by Christian scholars with regards to the authority of the Bible. Below is a summary based on Gnuse's work.

Verbal inspiration

The belief that the Bible came directly from God and was therefore without error, was fully developed during the nineteenth century, and won a strong following among conservative Protestants in the USA. The human authors of the Bible were regarded as prisms of glass through which God's light shone to create the rainbow of the biblical witness. If the Bible was a direct record of God's proclamation, it followed that there can be no errors in the text of the Bible, which led to much theological gymnastics to explain inconsistencies within the Bible or disagreements between Scripture and modern scientific knowledge (e.g. the challenge the theory of evolution presents to the creation stories of Genesis 1 and 2). Gnuse further notes that the belief in biblical inerrancy became more important to its followers than the Bible itself, 'so that a hedge must be placed around Scripture in order to protect it' (Gnuse 1985, p. 28).

Limited verbal inspiration

This theory retains a belief in the inspired nature of the Bible but limits it to core teaching about God and faith, allowing for the possibility of errors on scientific or historical matters since these were more likely to be influenced by the cultural context of the biblical authors. Gnuse suggests this model was dominant during the patristic period when the church's theology and creeds were debated and formalized. The major problem with this theory according to Gnuse is its inconsistency. How can we distinguish between human teaching and divine truths?

Non-textual inspiration

Scholars in this category suggest that the central ideas of the Bible were directly inspired but not the actual biblical text. Others believe the human authors of the Bible were inspired by God but their words were their own. This theory again fails to answer how we can identify these core ideas.

Social inspiration

This theory locates inspiration within the early communities of faith from which the Bible emerged. Christian communities with access to the apostolic witness remained open to divine inspiration during the creation of the New Testament. Gnuse notes how this approach fails to give sufficient importance to the creativity of individual authors.

This summary demonstrates the divergence of opinion about how the Bible can be said to be inspired. To complete Gnuse's survey, we should note that some Christians do not regard the Bible as a uniquely inspired text, believing that other texts or experiences are equally valid sources of knowledge about God and the world.

Try it out

Read John 2.1–11. Which of the previously listed understandings of the nature of the Bible is most helpful in your understanding of the passage? What type of authority (historical, moral, theological etc.) do you expect the Bible to have, if any?

Reading the Bible as a whole

The Bible is a collection of a number of books written in many different styles, in a range of contexts, over many centuries. We may wonder what binds the books of the Bible together so in this section we look at the formation of the biblical canon and its boundaries.

The biblical canons – variations on a theme

The word canon originates from a Greek word referring to a measuring rule or standard. In biblical studies 'canon' describes a set collection of books granted authoritative status by and for a particular community. These texts come from the formational period of the faith community and helped define it.

While it is usual to speak of the biblical canon, there is in fact no single agreed biblical canon. The Jewish community has its own canon know as the Tanakh. The word Tanakh refers to the three types of books included: *Torah* – Law, *Nebiim* – Prophets, and *Ketubim* – Writings. The collection includes the same 39 books that Christians recognize as the Hebrew Bible or Old Testament. (The 'law of Moses, the prophets, and the psalms' are referred to in Luke 24.44, for example, indicating the early church's continued acceptance of these collections.)

Within the Christian church, Catholic, Protestant and Orthodox Christians each accept the authority of slightly different numbers of books. The different versions are a result of different criteria (e.g. variant understandings of apostolic authorship); and different historical processes of formation. Each of these canons developed over time and through debate: for example, the book of Esther was a later addition to the Tanakh and there were centuries of discussion over the status of some of the letters that were eventually included in the New Testament. A useful comparison of the different canons can be found at the website of Felix Just SJ from Loyola Marymount University: http://myweb.lmu.edu/fjust/Bible/Heb-Xn-Bibles.htm

Try it out

Look at a copy of the Tanakh, a Protestant Bible with Apocrypha and a Catholic Bible. Compare the order of the canons and the value given to different sections of the canon (e.g. the value given to the Torah in the Tanakh). Look at any additional 'secondary status' books, e.g. in the Protestant Apocrypha. Then compare the version of Isaiah 42.1–9 given in each canon, noting different emphasis in the ordering, translation, or footnotes. What do you notice?

Canon formation

The different canons were established to mark boundaries and ensure orthodox teaching within particular communities. They were attempts to establish a particular identity, often in the face of internal or external threats. It is therefore not surprising that from the beginning there were disputes over the status of some books. The canons also reflect the context in which the collection was assembled, which often influenced how earlier texts were regarded.

For example, the Jewish community began to gather and authorize texts during the exile in Babylon during the sixth century BCE. This new context for the interpretation of the tradition had an impact on the final form of the Jewish canon. In the 1970s, James Saunders began to explore this issue. He questioned why the book of Joshua was excluded from the final form of the Torah, even though it appears to be a fulfilment of promises made earlier in the Torah. He suggested that the context of the Babylonian exile, where the shaping of the Torah took place, led to Joshua being left out of the most authoritative collection of books:

In Sanders' analysis, the canonical shaping of Israel's story into the Torah produced a radical new interpretation of the promise–fulfillment tradition by truncating the original story. For exiles in Babylon who had lost the land, the Torah offered a new reading of traditions that must have seemed dead, for it situated the fulfillment of the promise in the future. Further, the Torah moved the focus from the land, which Israel had lost, to the law, which it could never lose. (Callaway 1999, pp. 145–6)

For the early church, the formation of the New Testament involved several councils over a number of centuries. Felix Just lists the criteria on which the early church accepted books into the New Testament:

- Apostolic Origin – attributed to and based on the preaching/teaching of the first-generation apostles (or their close companions).
- Universal Acceptance – acknowledged by all major Christian communities in the ancient world (by the end of the fourth century).
- Liturgical Use – read publicly when early Christian communities gathered for the Lord's Supper (their weekly worship services).
- Consistent Message – containing a theological outlook similar or complementary to other accepted Christian writings.
  Taken from: http://myweb.lmu.edu/fjust/Bible/NT_Canon.htm#Canonicity

Elizabeth Schüssler Fiorenza, in a 1994 article 'Introduction: Transgressing Canonical Boundaries', points out the contested nature of the canon and the way canonical New Testament texts hide aspects of the life of the early church such as women's leadership. Indeed Schüssler Fiorenza suggests some of the texts that were eventually excluded from the New Testament may well have lost out because of their promotion of women's leadership roles, e.g. the Acts of Thecla (Schüssler Fiorenza 1994, pp. 8, 10). She has attempted to reconstruct women's roles in the early church to demonstrate the existence of an inclusive community of faith not given sufficient witness in the documents of the New Testament.

Motivations for canon formation were related to struggles for power and a desire for control. Once agreed, however, the Christian canons became authoritative for the church. Birch and Rasmussen suggest that the authority of the Bible for Christians is not located in the book itself but comes from the church's recognition of the importance of these writings:

> It is the recognition of the Christian community over centuries of experience that the Scripture is a source of empowerment for its life in the world. Authority derives from acknowledgment of a source's power to influence us, not from absolute power that operates apart from the affirmation of the community. (Birch and Rasmussen 1989, p. 142)

For this reason, scholars who use a canonical approach, notably Brevard Childs, are interested in the impact of reading the Bible as sacred Scripture. They look at how the community of faith interprets the texts so that a normative interpretation emerges. Moreover, they consider the mutual impact of the canon and the community, asking how the communities of faith and the developing traditions shaped each other.

Canonical approaches to the Bible encourage the Bible to be read as a whole, attending to the wider biblical context of each passage. These approaches consider how biblical texts work together to reinforce or modify each other. Such approaches are considered more fully in Chapter 5.

Canon formation was not restricted to selecting which books became part of the authorized collection. In the process of developing the canon, the early Jewish and Christian communities edited earlier writings and traditions, adapting them for their contemporary situation. This is particularly evident in the Hebrew Bible because of the lengthy time frame during which individual books were produced. Central events and stories are retold and reinterpreted throughout as new generations adapted traditional teaching to their own situation. Mary Calloway points out, 'The very nature of canon is to be simultaneously stable and adaptable, a fixed set of traditions infinitely adaptable to new contexts by successive communities of believers' (Callaway 1999, p. 146). Historical-critical methods, which study this process of adaptation and development, are dealt with in the next chapter.

Canonical diversity and intertextuality

The diverse nature of the canon provides readers with a colourful, multi-textured work with which to engage. For Christians, the inclusion of four

Gospels within the New Testament, for example, enriches their knowledge of Jesus and opens up space for them to enter into the traditions and events behind the four accounts.

When we compare different parts of the Bible we notice a variety of teaching, often in response to the differing circumstances of the faith communities from which the texts emerged. For example, the characters of Joseph and Daniel respond differently to life in foreign lands. Daniel holds fast to the teachings of his faith, refusing to eat food offered to idols or to worship the king. His actions lead him into the lions' den, from which he emerges unscathed thanks to his faithfulness (Dan. 6.6–28). In contrast, Joseph adapts a striking 'when in Rome' approach to life. He becomes Pharaoh's confidant, settles down in the life of the court and marries an Egyptian (Gen. 41.39–45). While Joseph's actions offered insight into how Jewish communities in strange lands (such as during the Babylonian exile) could thrive, Daniel's religious faithfulness encouraged later Jewish communities who wanted to retain their distinctiveness to survive in the long term.

The canon also enables us to use other biblical texts to help us interpret a particular passage. Gina Hens-Piazza reminds us:

> The collection was established on the consensus that together these books express the faith beliefs of communities claiming them as their confessional texts. 'Together' here is the operative word. The notion of canon is important for us because it suggests a further context for our story. It urges us to read and understand our tale *together* with other stories of the canon. (Hens-Piazza 2003, p. 96, Hens-Piazza's italics)

Hens-Piazza illustrates the benefits of reading a biblical text as part of the wider canon in her work on 2 Kings 6.24–33, the story of two cannibal mothers, King Jehoram and the prophet Elisha during the siege of Samaria. The brief yet disturbing story of the two women is explored with the help of other stories about two women, disputed children and powerful men – Sarah and Hagar (Gen. 16, 21.1–21), Rachel and Leah (Gen. 29–30), and the two prostitutes who appear before King Solomon (1 Kings 3.16–28).

Hens-Piazza draws fresh insights from reading the stories together, noting how in each story the women understand that children give them status, love and even life itself, and thus their struggle over children becomes more desperate. To contrast these four stories of bitter conflict between women, Hens-Piazza draws our attention to the beginning of Exodus, when co-operation between many women saves the newborn boy Moses in defiance of the destructive wishes of the Pharaoh. Hens-Piazza suggests that such courageous stories give readers hope and strengthen us to seek out alternate ways to the way of violence.

Beyond the canons: apocryphal, deuterocanonical and pseudepigraphical writings

There are many Jewish and early Christian texts that didn't quite make it into any of the canons. Some of these can be found in the Apocrypha, others in the Pseudepigrapha.

The Christian scholar Jerome (c. 345–420) defined the Jewish or Old Testament Apocrypha as those writings found in the Septuagint (the Greek version of Jewish biblical texts) but not in any Hebrew texts. A few apocryphal texts retained their canonical status in North African Christianity. Although Jerome identified these books as secondary or apocryphal, they continued to be widely used until the Reformation. The Protestant reformers with their emphasis on the authority of Scripture tightened up the boundaries of the canon and excluded these texts. However, some of these books retained their importance within the Catholic and Orthodox churches.

Consequently Catholics and Protestants refer to different books as the Apocrypha. When the Protestant reformers excluded much of the Catholic deuterocanon, these books became know as the Apocrypha. It is worth noting that the Protestant Apocrypha is not exactly the same as the Roman Catholic deuterocanonical books (Pyper 2000, p. 31).

In versions of the Bible that include the Apocrypha or the deuterocanonical books, these are listed according to their standing in each denomination. If you have such a version, you might find it useful to look at the contents page to gain an overview.

The Pseudepigrapha is a collection of Jewish and Christian writings (from as early as 650 BCE to as late as 800 CE but mostly written between 200 BCE and 200 CE) not awarded canonical or deuterocanonical status by the church. The writings of the Pseudepigrapha mostly emerged at a later stage than the deuterocanonical books, during what was to be a formative period for both Judaism and Christianity. It records a time of lively debate when these communities of faith were more receptive to influences from the surrounding cultures. Dominant themes include the origins of evil, the end of the world, the Messiah, angels and resurrection (Porter 2001, p. 8).

There is also a collection of books known as the Apocryphal New Testament that includes writings from the second to the ninth century; mostly of familiar genres such as letters, acts, gospels, for example, the Gospel of Thomas, the Acts of Andrew and the Protevangelium of James. These texts helped develop the status of the apostles and other early followers of Jesus. They often include more sensational miracles or stories. Various Christian doctrines about Mary originated in these apocryphal texts, notably the infancy gospels. Sometimes the texts increase Mary's standing, for example, claiming she also was a miracle worker, or embellish her earlier life, suggesting that she was brought up in the temple (Protevangelium of James). These stories about Mary illustrate the values of the second-century church and it is from this period, when celibacy was highly valued, that Mary's virginal status was upheld (Elliot 2000, pp. 30–1).

The non-canonical gospels have provoked the interest of feminist scholars who see in them possible signs of gender-inclusive early Christian communities. However, that these gospels give prominence to women disciples such as Mary Magdalene is not necessarily a sign of gender equality. Indeed, in the Gospel of Thomas (114.3) Mary Magdalene's entrance into the kingdom is dependent on her becoming male (although 'becoming male' could refer to keeping celibate; Økland 2001, p. 74). Nevertheless, like all excluded texts they offer alternative insights, here into the early church and patterns of discipleship.

With the growth of ecumenism and awareness of the historical influence of the Apocrypha, there has been a revival of interest in these texts. What do they offer us as biblical interpreters? They help us understand more about early Jewish and Christian communities, and the history of reception of canonical texts within these communities. They offer us imaginative extensions of familiar stories and fresh perspectives. And they can redress the balance of our understanding of the biblical witness, perhaps reminding us of the strong eschatological flavour of Judaism and Christianity during this time, something that can alienate contemporary readers who tend not to share some of the biblical writers' expectations of an imminent end to the world.

Changing the canon today

Inclusion in the biblical canon(s) awarded books authority in the life of the Jewish community and the church. At the same time, it had the effect of limiting Christian and Jewish understandings of revelation. It was as if God had stopped communicating with the world once the last canonical book was completed. The United Church of Christ challenges this view with its testimony that 'God is still speaking' echoing the Pilgrim pastor, John Robinson's encouragement that, 'God hath yet more light and truth to break forth from God's Holy Word.' The denomination believes that belief in ongoing revelation opens up space for Christians to respond to God in new ways that are relevant to today's needs. We could see this as a move to extend the canon to include people's lived experience as well as authoritative texts. The church's website is: www.stillspeaking.com

Some theologians advocate an extended written canon, arguing that we need to recognize the limitations of the canon. They point out that many people do not find themselves portrayed within the Bible, or only in negative ways. Therefore other stories need to be read alongside the Bible to redress the balance. Through this process, the experiences of contemporary and culturally diverse communities are allowed to interact with the biblical narrative that describes the experiences of the early Judeo-Christian community.

These alternative narratives are used to critique the Bible and provide new insights into the text and new ways of living. Among scholars from Asia, Africa and Latin America there has been a rise in academic interest in indigenous traditions and texts. As one of many examples, Musa Dube from Botswana uses a traditional story from her own community, that of

Utentelezandlane, a beautiful princess, to critique the biblical story of Judith (Dube 2003, p. 60). Similarly, Atabaque, a group of black pastoral workers in Brazil argue that:

> The Bible is one source among many. Sometimes it is not even the main one. For the poor and the black, the stories of the saints and of miracles stand side by side, for example, with the sung and danced stories of thee *terreiro* of Candomblé. The Bible of the *terreiro* is a story that is danced and sung. It is not written, it cannot be read ... but it is also a story of salvation and liberation. (Cited in Pereira 2003, p. 52)

As a further example of this process, feminist and African American women (womanist) scholars, in response to the lack of women's voices in the biblical canon, have advocated an extended canon that includes novels and literature written by and about women. A classic example of this is the importance of Alice Walker's novel, *The Color Purple* (1983), within womanist theology. Katie Cannon remarks how the oppressive use of the Bible and the limited insights it offers have created this need to read texts written by and about black women alongside the Bible. She comments, 'Canon formation is a way of establishing new and larger contexts of experience within which African American women can attend to the disparity between sources of oppression and sources for liberation' (Cannon 1995, p. 76).

Try it out

You may already have books, songs or films that might form part of your extended canon. These might be stories that resonate with your own experience or that have enabled you to see the world in a new way. Draw up your own extended canon and note the ways it allows you to make use of other resources in your biblical interpretation, theology or reflections on life.

Christian scholars such as Dube and Cannon do not reject the traditional canon but feel it needs to be opened up to include a wider range of experiences. Of course, such moves are vigorously contested by some other Christians who do not believe that the canon can or should be extended beyond the Bible. This is particularly true of Christians who believe the Bible represents a unique unrepeated revelation. William Abraham, an American Methodist scholar, explains why moves to extend or change the canon are so divisive:

> In a real sense canonical material is actually constituted by the community. The two ideas, canon and community, are logically and reciprocally related. A community constitutes its canonical heritage, and in doing so, that community is itself constituted along certain lines. That is one reason why the development of canonical material and its subsequent rejection is so significant for a community. Once a community has formed its canonical traditions, changing, transforming, or rejecting those traditions from within is liable to be a convulsive affair. (Abraham 1998, p. 30)

However, Abraham himself argues that the canonical heritage of the church should not be limited to Scripture since it was always wider than that, including canon law, church councils and the embodied wisdom of cathedral canons. This breadth enables him to see the canon is a place of encounter with God rather than a measuring rule against which to judge other pronouncements about God (Abraham 1998, p. 474).

Other scholars who advocate an entirely open canon, 'declare the canonization process of the fourth century a mistake or failure of nerve' (Gnuse 1985, p. 95). They argue that the formation of the canon was a theological or political act of control, undertaken in response to perceived heresies or other threats. All canons by their very nature are exclusive and therefore suspect. On the other hand, an open canon removes any control the church might have over what understandings of God are acceptable within it.

Try it out

What do you think are the advantages to an open canon? How does opening up the canon affect the shape of a community of faith that traditionally held to a fixed canon?

Favouring parts of the Bible

Stephen Dawes points out:

> The Bible does not interpret itself; it is not self-explanatory. There is even a sense in which the Bible is silent, that it cannot speak for itself and that its users give it the only voice it has. The Bible is, after all, a book. No matter how venerable it is, it has to be opened and its chapters and verses selected before they can be quoted and used. (Dawes 2004, p. 114)

In this section, we will examine how readers select passages from the Bible for study, worship or other purposes. Many of us have favourite passages of Scripture, the ones we turn to for insight and guidance. The Jewish community and Christian church also have their favourites, those books that are regarded as central to God's revelation. The Torah and the Gospels are both placed at the start of the Tanakh and New Testament respectively, immediately indicating their primary importance. They are the books through which the other books in the collection are to be understood. *The Jewish Study Bible* notes, 'In Judaism, the Torah is accorded the highest level of sanctity, above that of the other books of the Bible' (Berlin and Brettler 2004, p. 1). Furthermore, Jewish and Christian worship will always include a reading from the Torah or Gospels correspondingly. The predominance of these texts is clear. They include the foundational stories of each faith community – the acts of creation, exodus and blessing; and the incarnation. As one such foundational event, the exodus is rehearsed time and time again in the biblical narrative. It represents the defining moment in Israel's relationship with God, and no matter what difficulties Israel experiences, this story retains the power to strengthen and shape the community. It is not only Jewish readers who hold the exodus as a foundation event, early Latin American liberation theology was also heavily reliant on the exodus narrative in which God hears and responds to the cries of the oppressed.

Try it out

Rank these books in order of importance: Matthew, Genesis, Numbers, Ruth, Habakkuk, Titus, Romans.

What criteria did you use to order the books? You may have used one of the following criterion: influence on the church or society, length, date, reference to Jesus.

We all inevitably favour some stories, characters or books of the Bible over others. Within Christian history, this favouring of certain texts has shaped the theological understanding of different groups. In his mission to uphold 'justification by faith' rather than 'justification by works', Luther famously dismissed the letter of James as an 'epistle of straw'! It could be argued that Luther's dislike for James moved social action or 'good works' to a marginal position in the theology of the emerging Protestant church.

Try it out

Do you turn to some biblical books more frequently than others? Would you disregard any books, perhaps some of the more obscure prophecies or letters? What about in your academic course or church – which texts are given priority there?

In the 1930s some German theologians, building on the work of liberal scholars such as Adolf von Harnack (1851–1930), promoted a truncated version of the Bible that contained no reference to the Old Testament, which was regarded as a Jewish book contrary to the New Testament. This denial of the Jewish roots of Christianity was part of the wider anti-Semitic movement that led ultimately to the Shoah (destruction) or Holocaust. The *Deutsche Christen* or 'German Christians' were accused of Marcionism, a heresy named after Marcion, who in the second century rejected the Old Testament (as well as much of the New Testament, retaining only Luke and ten epistles) as a valid part of the Christian Scriptures. In fact, it was in his work on Marcion that von Harnack suggested it was time to review the canonical status of the Old Testament.

This is an extreme example of the way all readers inevitably favour some books of the Bible. We naturally prefer stories that inspire us or characters we relate to. What we need to ensure, however, is that the Bible is understood as a whole, as a rich and diverse testimony of faith. Those unfamiliar stories may be the ones through which we can encounter God again in new and surprising ways.

Reading systematically through the whole canon: The use of a lectionary in worship

Following long-established Jewish practice, the early church drew up a scheme for the use of biblical passages during worship. Many Christian denominations today continue this practice, ordering their reading of the Bible to ensure key texts are heard by the congregation at least once every year or over a number of years on a rolling cycle. By using an agreed lectionary in a local church, biblical passages are encountered in a systematic way.

There are benefits to this process: it disciplines worship leaders to make use of a wider range of biblical texts than ones they are familiar or comfortable with; it enables churches to plan ahead and work with other local churches across denominations who use the same lectionary (for example, through *Roots*, an ecumenical worship and learning resource www.rootsontheweb. com); it adds to the structure and order of the church year; it helps worship leaders make connections between biblical texts.

The Revised Common Lectionary (RCL) is a three-year cycle of Bible readings developed in 1992 by the Consultation on Common Texts (a North American-based organization but with international connections: visit www.commontexts.org for more details). In Britain, the RCL is used in many Methodist and United Reformed Churches locally. The Church of England adapted the RCL to produce the *Common Worship* lectionary. The Roman Catholic Church also has its own lectionary but there are many points of contact between this and the RCL:

> The Revised Common Lectionary http://divinity.library.vanderbilt.edu/lectionary/

> The Church of England *Common Worship* Lectionary http://www.cofe.anglican.org/commonworship/lect/lectfront1.html

The *Book of Common Prayer* Lectionary http://www.cofe.anglican.org/commonworship/lect/bcp/lectfront.html

The RCL responded to calls from the churches for more exposure to the historical books and wisdom literature of the Hebrew Scriptures. It focuses on the patriarchal/Mosaic narrative for Year A (Matthew), the Davidic narrative for Year B (Mark), and the Elijah/Elisha/Minor Prophets series for Year C (Luke).

Use of a lectionary may, however, restrict worship leaders and prevent them from responding to dynamics within the local church or to news and current events. A further concern about the uncritical use of a lectionary is that worship leaders and congregations may be guided towards particular interpretations of a text through the placing of certain texts together. For example, for the fourth Sunday in Advent in Year A, Isaiah 7.10–16, Isaiah's prophecy about a young woman with child is set with the birth of Jesus in Matthew 1.18–25. Such groupings suggest to preachers and worship leaders that a reading from the Hebrew Scriptures should be interpreted through the lens of the Gospel reading it is linked with for that Sunday. Another obvious difficulty is that the Christian lectionaries do not include the whole Bible, even over a three-year cycle. If Christians only hear Scripture read on a Sunday, the lectionary acts as a filter to their comprehension of the Bible, shaping their understanding of the priorities of Christianity. So which passages are heard over and over in church? Which stories is the contemporary church embarrassed by, and does this give the church the right to ignore them?

As one example, the RCL includes just two readings from Judges: Judges 4.1–7 (part of the story of Deborah) and Judges 6.11–24 (part of Gideon's story). More challenging texts, texts that vividly describe violent acts or questionable characters, such as Ehud's trickery and murder of King Eglon (Judges 3.15–25) or Jael's role in the victory of Deborah and Barak, through the murder of Sisera with a tent peg (Judges 4.17–22), do not appear in the lectionary. Similarly, the teaching concerning the relationship between wives and husbands, and slaves and masters from Ephesians is not in the lectionary. The silence over such problematic texts can be unhelpful since it reduces the opportunities for debate of traditional interpretations.

Try it out

Look up the set readings for the forthcoming Sunday in the RCL or another lectionary. Read the set readings and, if it is a festival season rather than Ordinary Time, look at what connections are implied by the grouping of the texts on this particular Sunday. What understanding of each text is encouraged by this process? Do you agree with it? How would you explain or challenge such interpretations?

Listening to marginalized texts and silent voices

In the life of the church, synagogue or university, we spend more time with a few texts than with many others. It is through these central texts that we learn much about the key beliefs of faith communities. However, we will not get the whole story from concentrating on these favoured texts alone. Sometimes we need to search around at the edges of the Bible to discover new images of God and the world. To redress the balance, some biblical scholars, particularly those working from a feminist commitment, prioritize lesser known passages and characters, and even spend time with the silences of the text. In these places and spaces, there are hints of alternative communities and understandings of God that have been suppressed and denied.

The Bible is an attempt by a believing community to offer reflections about God's relationship with it. At times the people write as those with much power and at other times as a community with little power. Most often it is the powerful within the community whose views are recorded but there are also critiques of the dominant story, such as the witness of the prophets. Often, in order to build up a fuller picture of the community's experience of God, we have to consider who or what is absent from the text.

An important example of this reconstructive work is Elisabeth Schüssler Fiorenza's *In Memory of Her: A Feminist Theological Reconstruction of Christian Origins* (1983). Through careful investigation, Fiorenza builds up an alternative picture of the early Christian community in which women played a full part. The presence of female leaders in the earliest house churches, offer a strong model of inclusivity for the contemporary church today. This reconstruction of the church's beginnings challenges the continued patriarchy of the church.

Try it out

Read through either the book of Obadiah or the letter of Jude. Now answer the following questions about this text:

- Who is present or absent? (think about communities or groups as well as individuals)
- How is the story or event told? What is the narrative slant? What value judgements are made by the narrator, speaker or writer?
- Why do you think this text has been left on the fringes of the canon?
- What connections can you spot between this text and other texts in the canon?
- How does this text balance other texts or movements within the canon, i.e. why might it have been included in the canon?

Unity in diversity?

As we come to the end of this section on the biblical canons, let us return to the questions with which we began this section: What binds these diverse texts together? And how do we understand difference or tension within the Bible?

Some readers do not acknowledge any fundamental divergence of thought within the Bible. Brevard Childs' canonical approach describes the whole canon as the arena for understanding. He and others who follow his approach, believe that the full canon must be held together. There can be a lively discussion between the different voices but all must be heard:

> The most significant theological contribution of canonical criticism is the axiom that no voice of the canon should be privileged over others: there is no text by which all other texts must be interpreted. Biblical texts only become the Word of God in their full canonical context. (Callaway 1999, p. 150)

Other interpreters question whether this attempt at unity is successful and argue that canonical approaches effectively push for the establishment of standard or approved interpretations, limiting the possibilities for other critical or fresh readings.

In these postmodern times, some interpreters argue that the plurality and tensions of the biblical narratives are both realistic and liberative. Walter Brueggemann suggests that the time for 'thin readings' is at an end and we should rejoice in the density of the text (Brueggemann 1997b, p. 61). Through the tension, dialogue and spaces within the material, there is room for much creativity and the emergence of many stories and many more readings of them. Brueggemann argues that the Bible itself points beyond any exclusive reading, Christian, Jewish or other; noting that even the original and still valid Jewish interpretations of the Hebrew Bible must allow room for other readings alongside them:

> In the text, there is a recurring restlessness about a Jewish reading and a push beyond that to a reading as large as the nations and as comprehensive as creation ... The text simply will not be contained in any such vested reading, which is what makes the text both compelling and subversive. (Brueggemann 1997b, p. 95)

Try it out

What tensions have you experienced within the Bible? Do you seek to resolve them, and if so, how?

As we end this chapter, it is time to focus in on a text you are currently working on, for an assignment, sermon or some other reason.

Try it out

Thinking of a biblical text you are working with, ask yourself:
- How familiar is this text to you and your community?
- What do you already know about it?
- Is it a text that you are comfortable with, or do you have some concerns or questions? What are they?

- What are your expectations about the text? Are you searching for an answer to a particular question or resources to 'prove' an argument? How open are you to discovering something contradictory or unexpected?
- How much are you prepared to challenge the text from your own life experience?

3

Tools for exegesis

Learning to do exegesis

Somewhere along the line, every biblical interpreter has to deal with the fact that the text before her or him is an old one: written or compiled on the basis of earlier oral or written traditions, in an ancient language and in a culture very different from the western world of the twenty-first century.

It is a collection of classic texts, a bit like the works of Shakespeare, though Shakespeare is much, much nearer us in time and culture, and wrote all the plays himself – in English. As a collection of classic texts, the Bible has already had a long history of interpretation in our culture and has influenced the way we think, speak and even behave. Most chapters in this book make some reference to the importance of this impact on history.

This chapter deals with exegesis, demonstrating some of the tools and approaches that help us engage more systematically with whatever Bible passage is before us. There is nothing mysterious about this. It is just a matter of learning to use skills and tools, some of which we will already have: a bit like learning to do DIY or a craft.

Terms such as 'exegesis' can be intimidating, but they needn't be. Every discipline has its own special technical language and biblical interpretation is no exception. Words like 'exegesis' and 'hermeneutics' are just technical words for everyday concepts. 'Exegesis' simply means a careful systematic study of a passage using a range of methods, and 'hermeneutics' is another word for interpretation. Exegesis is an important part of the whole process of biblical interpretation, but it is not the whole of it, nor its starting point, as is obvious from the placement of this chapter some way into the overall book.

When we do an exegesis of a biblical passage we consider it from two points of view:

- First, we have a good look at it as it is, here and now.
- Next, we investigate how it came to be here, in this form, in this place in the Bible.

This distinction between looking at a text as it is and as it has developed was borrowed by biblical scholars from structural linguistics. The technical words for these viewpoints are synchronic (with time) and diachronic (through time). The distinction enables us to be clear in our own minds about whether we are thinking about the final form of the passage in front of us, or thinking about the history of its development.

This is one example of the way exegesis makes use of tools for studying ancient texts borrowed from other disciplines, such as history or literature. Each tool has a different purpose and orientation. Some are designed to help us explore the history of the formation of the passage spotting, for example, where a quotation from another writer has been inserted. Other tools help us appreciate the artistic skill of the author or editor. This chapter will introduce you to some of these tools and help you to begin to use them for yourself.

Synchronic approaches

When we take a synchronic approach to a passage we look at the final form of a biblical text. We do so knowing that the text has a long history of development and that close historical work on the formation of this text and later on its history of transmission underlies the 'final form' of the text before us. But we set this aside for the moment, and just look at the text before us as it is, as language and as literature.

Considering the text as language, we draw on the tools of structural linguistics to see how the text has been structured, combining particular words together into sentences and larger sense units. There is nothing mysterious about this either: we simply look at the way the passage before us either follows, or departs from, the conventions of Greek or Hebrew literature and grammar of that time. The way the text conveys meaning through the way it has been structured is obviously important. Here we look at how the text conveys meaning not just through its words and grammar, but also through the patterns and relationships within and between smaller and larger parts of the text. This disciplined examination of the way the text is organized often yields exciting insights into its meaning.

Reading a Bible passage as literature means reading it just as carefully as we do any other literature. Much of this involves the same common-sense decisions we make every time we read anything. We first decide what kind of text it is (its genre or form) to enable us to read it appropriately. Reading a text as literature involves attending to its shape, structure and flow (how it has been composed), its theme, plot and character development, and the way it makes its impact upon us. It may try to surprise us, as many of Jesus' parables do; to persuade us, as Paul frequently does using all his skills of argument; or to disorientate and inspire us, as does the book of Revelation with its strange structure and bizarre imagery.

When we look at the final form of a text, we look first at it as language and literature, using approaches developed from modern linguistics and literary criticism. Many other modern disciplines also provide us with lenses which we can use to read the text in its final form: geography, history in all areas (social, military, political, scientific, philosophical, moral, etc.), models developed in the social sciences (particularly anthropology, sociology and psychology), philosophy, biology, politics, art, film and media studies and so on. None of these can be ignored today but, as the Bible presents itself to us as a written text, logically we have to begin by reading it as language and literature.

This is enough theory for the moment. Let us begin to do some exegesis. In this chapter we will be working with a few longer examples to see how the critical tools work together.

Making the text our own

The first requirement of exegesis is to make the text our own, at least in a preliminary way. Hans-Ruedi Weber, an experienced leader of group Bible studies for the World Council of Churches, offers a number of suggestions for doing this in an excellent guide to group Bible study called *The Book that Reads Me* (1995). The first chapter of this book reminds us that before the Bible was written down, much of it was communicated from person to person orally. Because of this oral dimension to the Bible, one simple way of getting a fresh grasp of a biblical text is to read it aloud. This helps us to hear the rhythms of the text or to appreciate where and why there are patterns or repetitions to help listeners to follow. Other ways in which we can experience a biblical passage afresh, and do justice to its oral character are by memorizing it, retelling it or even singing it (Weber 1995, pp.1–6).

Yet, we are now much more familiar with the Bible as a written text. Over a long period, the oral traditions in the Bible were recorded, revised and expanded in written form. Even after the canon was substantially complete, for most of the Bible's lifetime, copies of the Bible were made by hand. Copying out a Bible passage by hand is another good way of hearing it afresh.

Try it out

The story of the Tower of Babel is well known and has a long impact history. An internet image search produces hundreds of artists' impressions of the tower, used for all sorts of purposes. But what do you remember of the whole story? As we have done earlier, begin by making a few notes (or even a little sketch) on what you recall of this story.

Now turn to Genesis 11.1–9 and write it out in your own handwriting. As you write, you may notice things that you want to find out more about, for example:

- What understanding of the 'whole earth' does the writer presuppose? Is Genesis 10 presupposed?
- Who are 'they' in v. 2 and are they moving to or from the east? (See the note in the margin of the New Revised Standard Version.)
- Where is Shinar, in relation to 'the whole earth'?

You may also ask questions about the character of the Lord in this story, e.g., Why does it think of the Lord as having to 'come down' to see the city and tower? Come down from where? Can the Lord not see everywhere? Why is the Lord apparently against human achievement?

After copying out the passage, look back at your notes or sketch of what you thought the story was about. How accurate was your recollection of it?

Discourse analysis

Despite the value of using handwriting to make a text our own, a computer is an invaluable aid for biblical studies. This enables us to have access to a wide range of Bible translations and to cut and paste passages for study into our own word processor. For the next part of this section we shall use an electronic text of Genesis 11.1–9 to illustrate how to analyse the structure and composition of a passage in more detail with discourse analysis.

Discourse analysis is a very useful tool for looking closely at the surface structure of a passage, helping us to pay close attention to the way a passage is 'joined up' grammatically and stylistically. It arose in the early 1970s and was developed by South African and American biblical scholars who were influenced by developments in linguistics and Bible translation. Initially some thought that it might provide them with a scientific way of determining *the* structure of a passage. Later, as it became clear that scholars continued to offer different analyses of the structure of the same text, it was recognized that it was simply a useful descriptive tool: a way of looking. While it is not the only exegetical tool biblical interpreters have borrowed from linguistics, it is one of the most useful. It enables us to explain, to ourselves and then to others, how we read the text: how we understand it to be organized and how this affects what we understand it to mean.

This description might still sound complicated. So, here is an extended example of how it works in practice. First, obtain an electronic copy of the passage in the New Revised Standard Version (NRSV) translation. A copy of this, with many other translations, and the facility to study them side by side, is available from: http://bible.crosswalk.com. If internet access is not avaliable, CD-ROMs with multiple Bible translations are available to buy.

> *1* Now the whole earth had one language and the same words. *2* And as they migrated from the east, they came upon a plain in the land of Shinar and settled there. *3* And they said to one another, 'Come, let us make bricks, and burn them thoroughly.' And they had brick for stone, and bitumen for mortar. *4* Then they said, 'Come, let us build ourselves a city, and a tower with its top in the heavens, and let us make a name for ourselves; otherwise we shall be scattered abroad upon the face of the whole earth.'
>
> *5* The Lord came down to see the city and the tower, which mortals had built. *6* And the Lord said, 'Look, they are one people, and they have all one language; and this is only the beginning of what they will do; nothing that they propose to do will now be impossible for them. *7* Come, let us go down, and confuse their language there, so that they will not understand one another's speech.' *8* So the Lord scattered them abroad from there over the face of all the earth, and they left off building the city. *9* Therefore it was called Babel, because there the Lord confused the language of all the earth; and from there the Lord scattered them abroad over the face of all the earth.

Having cut and pasted this text from a source like this, the next stage is to divide the text into smaller sense units. The aim here is to release the text from the later additions of chapter and verse numbering. (We retain the verse numbering for ease of cross-reference though.)

Now, identify the main verbs. In the example below, the verbs are highlighted in bold. (Remember that sometimes a verb is made up of more than one word, such as 'will be impossible'. Also, infinitives (like 'to see' or 'to do') are verbal nouns. As the subject or object of other verbs they do the work of nouns and so are not counted as verbs.)

> *1* Now the whole earth **had** one language and the same words. *2* And as they **migrated** from the east, they **came** upon a plain in the land of Shinar and **settled** there. *3* And they **said** to one another, '**Come**, let us **make** bricks, and **burn** them thoroughly.' And they **had** brick for stone, and

bitumen for mortar. *4* Then they **said**, 'Come, **let** us **build** ourselves a city, and a tower with its top in the heavens, and **let** us **make** a name for ourselves; otherwise we **shall be scattered** abroad upon the face of the whole earth.'

5 The Lord **came** down to see the city and the tower, which mortals **had built**. *6* And the Lord **said**, 'Look, they **are** one people, and they **have** all one language; and this **is** only the beginning of what they **will do**; nothing that they **propose** to do **will** now **be impossible** for them. *7* Come, **let** us **go** down, and **confuse** their language there, so that they **will** not **understand** one another's speech.' *8* So the Lord **scattered** them abroad from there over the face of all the earth, and they **left** off building the city. *9* Therefore it **was called** Babel, because there the Lord **confused** the language of all the earth; and from there the Lord **scattered** them abroad over the face of all the earth.

Marking up the verbs has two purposes. First, it is necessary for the next step when we divide the text up further into separate lines (called cola). Second, it helps our understanding by drawing our attention to key actions within the passage. Here these are: migration and settlement, brick-making and building, scattering and confusion.

Third, divide the text up further into cola, with just one verb on each line:

1 Now the whole earth **had** one language and the same words.
2 And as they **migrated** from the east,
they **came** upon a plain in the land of Shinar
and **settled** there.
3 And they **said** to one another,
'Come,
let us **make** bricks,
and **burn** them thoroughly.'
And they **had** brick for stone, and bitumen for mortar.
4 Then they **said**,
'Come,
let us **build** ourselves a city, and a tower with its top in the heavens,

and **let** us **make** a name for ourselves;
otherwise we **shall be scattered** abroad upon the face of the whole earth.'
5 The Lord **came** down to see the city and the tower,
which mortals **had built**.
6 And the Lord **said**,
'**Look**,
they **are** one people,
and they **have** all one language;
and this **is** only the beginning
of what they **will do**;
nothing that they **propose** to do
will now **be impossible** for them.
7 **Come**,
let us **go** down,
and **confuse** their language there,
so that they **will** not **understand** one another's speech.'
8 So the Lord **scattered** them abroad from there over the face of all the earth,
and they **left off** building the city.
9 Therefore it **was called** Babel,
because there the Lord **confused** the language of all the earth;
and from there the Lord **scattered** them abroad over the face of all the earth.

Fourth, mark up the linguistic structure of the passage. Begin by separating with another line space the lines that ought to stand on their own as completely distinct statements.

Then show the relative position of lines that belong together with indents. So, for example, the layout of verse 3 below indents the different parts of what they said, and what they had. What they said belongs together, first that they said something, then the summons itself 'Come', and then two further parts, the summon to make bricks, and a detail about how they would make them. The square bracket before certain indented words just indicates that the line above is continued below.

Next, mark the subjects of each sentence. Here they are underlined. This helps to make clear where there is a change of subject. For example, the subject changes from 'the whole earth' in verse 1 to 'they' in verses 2–4. In verses 5–7 the subject changes again to 'the Lord'. Verse 8 either continues this unit or follows it, as indicated by 'so' – more investigation is needed! Verse 9 with the subject of the city/tower 'it' is a summary verse. Insert a dotted line to mark these changes of subject. This corresponds roughly with the idea of reasons for starting a new paragraph. The reason 'the Lord came' and 'the Lord scattered' might be marked as separate sections is that it helps to show how the section in which the Lord scatters the people (v. 8) has a relationship with the people's motivation for building the tower, their fear of being scattered, in verse 4.

1 Now <u>the whole earth</u> **had** one language and the same
              [words.

....

2 And as <u>they</u> **migrated** from the east,
    <u>they</u> **came** upon a plain in the land of Shinar
    and **settled** there.

3 And <u>they</u> **said** to one another,
    '**Come,**
        let us **make** bricks,
            and **burn** them thoroughly.'

And <u>they</u> **had** brick for stone, and bitumen for mortar.

4 Then <u>they</u> **said,**
    '**Come,**
        let us **build** ourselves a city, and a tower with its
            [top in the heavens,
        and **let** us **make** a name for ourselves;
        otherwise we **shall be scattered** abroad upon
        the face of the
            [whole earth.'

....

5 <u>The Lord</u> **came** down to see the city and the tower,
    which mortals **had built**.

6 And <u>the Lord</u> **said**,
    '**Look**,
        they **are** one people,
        and they **have** all one language;
        and this **is** only the beginning
        of what they **will do**;
        nothing that they **propose** to do
        will now **be impossible** for them.

7   **Come**,
        let <u>us</u> **go** down,
        and **confuse** their language there,
        so that they **will not understand** one another's
            [speech.'

....

8 So <u>the Lord</u> **scattered** them abroad from there over the
            [face of all the earth,
and they **left** off building the city.

....

9 Therefore <u>it</u> **was called** Babel,
    because there the Lord **confused** the language of all
        [the earth;
    and from there the Lord **scattered** them abroad
        [over the face of all the earth.

Fifth, use coloured pens to mark recurrent words and phrases in different colours. In this example, we have already noticed the important verbs ('migration' and 'settlement', 'brick-making' and 'building', 'scattering' and 'confusion') and subjects ('the whole earth', 'they', 'the Lord' and 'the city'). Now, using coloured pens, we identify other recurrent words and phrases.

Here they are:

> 'The whole earth' (v. 1, v. 4, v 8 and v. 9, in each of the sections)
> 'Language' (v. 1, v. 6, v. 7 and v. 9)
> 'City' and 'tower' (v. 4 and v. 5)
> 'Building' (v. 4 and v. 8)

The passage is divided in half by the almost exact repetition of 'scattered abroad upon the face of the whole earth' at the end of verse 4 and 'scattered them abroad over the face of all the whole earth' at the end of verse 9.

Discourse analysis is a very useful tool to aid our reading. At this point, without reference to any other study aids, we are able to give reasons for our understanding of:

- the shape of the passage, with a sense of how it is organized (initial situation v.1; human action in vv. 2–4 opposed by the Lord in vv. 5–7; the Lord's response to the human desire to make a name for themselves; vv. 8–9 outcome and commentary);
- the themes of the passage, with a sense of what is repeatedly stated (settlement, building and scattering);
- subjects of the passages;
- and their actions.

Note that discourse analysis alone cannot tell us what this information signified to earlier readers, or what this information will eventually signify for us, but it does help to give us a grip on the text.

By beginning to observe closely what is there (and what is not) we are freed from earlier preconceptions. For example, there is little or no indication that the human desire to build arose from a deliberate attempt to oppose or emulate God. The text states that it arose from the builders' desire to make a name for themselves and their fear of being scattered. The text indicates that the Lord opposed this. As interpreters we are now left to seek the answer why. To do so, we have to move beyond looking at the surface of the text to listening to the story which it tells. This involves a shift of perspective from looking at the passage from the outside to looking at it from within.

Moving on: From linguistic to literary approaches

The other major synchronic approach to the passage is to read it as literature. There are many literary critical methods available to answer all sorts of questions:

- What is the place of this passage within the biblical book as a whole?
- What sort of writing is it? Is it history or legend, for example? How does this affect the way we are expected to read it?
- What sort of narrative techniques are used, e.g. does the passage use direct or indirect speech? What other techniques are used to portray the characters?
- Is there a particular significance to the sequence of the events in the passage?
- Are there any obvious persuasive strategies 'encoded' within the narrative? What techniques is the narrator of this tale using to persuade his/her hearers to believe or do?

While it is useful to ask such questions of smaller passages, such as the Genesis 11.1–9 above, literary approaches are particularly helpful for getting a grip on longer passages, of which there are many in the Bible, e.g. in the books of Judges, Samuel and Kings in the Hebrew Bible, or in Acts or Revelation in the New Testament. Literary criticism, in the sense that we use it below, has been very helpful in allowing Bible interpreters to see larger patterns and relationships within and between books of the Bible.

Narrative criticism

Literary criticism covers a wide range of critical approaches that read the final form of the text from the perspective of particular groups of readers. Understood thus, it includes such reader-orientated methods as deconstruction, feminist criticism, political criticism, psychoanalytic criticism and reader-response criticism (Gunn 1999, p. 210).

We look at some of these tools in Chapter 5. Here we use narrative criticism to concentrate on 'the story being told' (Soulen and Soulen 2001, pp. 119–20). Narrative criticism in this narrower sense asks us to identify the plot, the characters, the place and time of the events presented, and so on. It attends to the way the story is told, the author's perspective as revealed within the text, and indicators of what the author expected of the readers. As much of the Bible is in the form of narrative, narrative criticism is an important tool for biblical interpretation.

As with other critical tools, this approach also uses technical language, but its focus is helpful. It sets aside all historical questions about the text: authorship, readership, time of writing, reasons for writing and so on, and focuses on getting into the story itself. It requires us to begin with the obvious: to respect narratives for what they are and to read them as narratives. Obviously this is not 'the whole story', but equally, unless we read stories as stories, we will never hear the whole story.

Narrative criticism is best kept simple. Alert watchers of thrillers on film or TV have already got all the necessary skills! For the sake of completeness, here is a fairly full list of the kind of things that narrative critics look for when reading (for more details, see Powell 1999, pp. 244–8). These are used below to study the account of Paul's shipwreck in Acts 27.

The events

Ordering of events

Narratives normally expect readers to bear in mind what has gone before. Sometimes events are presented out of order for dramatic effect. Many film thrillers do this, for example.

Length/frequency of events

Narratives give emphasis to events by giving more detail or repeatedly describing an event. Think of the expansion of detail in the Gospel passion narratives.

Links between events

Is what is happening linked to something that has happened, or is going to happen?

Where and when the events take place

These details may or may not be significant. A man takes off his trousers. Whether this is noteworthy is determined by whether he does this in the bathroom, just before taking a bath, or in the boardroom, just before giving a presentation!

Conflict

Most good narratives involve conflict, and there are many examples of this in the Bible. What will God do after Adam and Eve disobey? Will Moses get the people through the Red Sea in time? Will Pilate acquit or condemn Jesus? Sometimes the narrative goes on to answer our questions; sometimes it leaves us to fill in the gaps. The incomplete ending of Mark's Gospel begs the question: Did Mark intend this, or has some of the manuscript been lost?

Try it out

Practise using these categories, and those below, by using them to analyse a short television drama or sitcom.

The characters

It is essential to identify who the characters are in a narrative. Again, if we think of televised or live drama, TV guides list the characters as an aid to the viewers and theatre programmes serve the same function for playgoers. Such guides tell us who the characters are, listing them in order of appearance or importance. We expect these characters to develop through what happens in the narrative. Minor characters often do not develop and may be portrayed in a stereotypical way: tough policeman, anxious mum, and so on.

So, for example, if you were studying characterization in the Gospel of Mark, you would look at: Jesus, the Roman and Jewish authorities, the disciples (the Twelve and other friends and followers) and the people (the crowds, the 'common people', and the multitudes). You would notice that Mark brings these characters to life by showing them, rather than describing them and by allowing them to develop as characters as the Gospel unfolds. To investigate matters more closely you would also consider:

- the viewpoint, motivation and values of the characters;
- whether they are named or unnamed;
- where they live, their place in society and their gender;
- what they say and do, and what others say and do to them;
- and, how they respond to the central character, Jesus.

The narrator

Narratives have narrators. Narrative critics are not concerned with who actually constructed the narrative historically, but with whose voice is heard within the narrative. Even a narrative that has been built up from the contributions of many authors and written sources has a perspective. Narrative critics attend to the values, beliefs and views of this 'implied author'.

In literature, the perspective of the implied author may or may not be trustworthy. This raises problems for biblical interpreters: Can the perspective of biblical narrators always be relied upon? As we have already seen in the example from Genesis 11.1–9, God often appears as a character in biblical narratives. Literary critics do not agree on whether God's viewpoint is normative for truth, as Mark Allen Powell asserts (1999, p. 246). By raising the question of the reliability of perspectives within narratives, narrative criticism invites readers to make their own considered judgements about these matters on the basis of their reading.

In literary criticism the narrator is the 'voice' inside the narrative telling the story. The actual identity of the person or persons who wrote or compiled the narrative is a different historical question which does not affect this. In fact, books of the Bible often fail to name the author explicitly. Also, ancient writers sometimes wrote pseudonymously, that is using the names of more famous biblical characters. The practice is found in the Hebrew Bible (e.g. Daniel), the Apocrypha and Pseudepigrapha (e.g. the Wisdom of Solomon), the New Testament (e.g. 2 Peter) and the New Testament Apocrypha. This was not done to deceive readers but to honour and extend the teaching of the person whose name was used. For example, by writing in the name of the apostle Peter, the author of 2 Peter claims to be a faithful mediator of the apostolic message (Bauckham 1983, pp. 161–2).

Literary strategies

As with all literature, biblical narratives use various literary devices in the course of telling their stories. They may describe symbolic language, actions or locations. In Genesis 11, what do the people in Babel mean when they say, 'Let us make a name for ourselves' (v. 4), what does their city with its tower with its top in the heavens symbolize, and is Shinar a significant place?

Narrators may also use irony. In the Babel story, the actions of the builders of the city and the tower achieves the exact opposite of what they intended. They are scattered. They make a name for themselves, but it is not the sort of reputation they wanted.

Biblical narrators often use intertexuality. This technical term simply recognizes that narratives often assume that their readers are familiar with other narratives. Biblical narrators often assume knowledge of other stories both within and outside the Bible. The Gospels assume that their readers know many parts of the Hebrew Bible. The stories of Elijah in Kings often remind readers of the stories of Moses, for example. Narrative critics draw attention to such intertexuality, and suggest that this points to the narrative unity of the whole of Genesis to 2 Kings.

Implied readers and the narrative world

Narrative critics also identify the persuasive thrust of a story by using the concept of implied readers. As with the implied author, this refers to an aspect of the narrative itself. This idea of the narrative's implied readers helps us to consider the way the narrative appears to expect readers to respond to its unfolding story. It enables us to think about how the narrative expects to influence the value judgements, beliefs and perceptions of its readers (Soulen and Soulen 2001, p.120). This may well not be what happens in reality. Once we become aware of how the text is trying to persuade or direct us, we are in a better position to decide whether we want to go along with this process, or resist it.

As readers we also need to distinguish the 'real world' from the 'narrative world' which is presented in the text. The narrative world is constructed by the person telling the story and is shaped by his/her values and beliefs. Think, for example, of the narrative world of a romantic novel or film: true love wins through in the novel or film in ways that don't often happen in the real world. Individual narrators may follow or depart from such conventions in constructing the particular narrative world of the story they are telling.

An extended example: Paul's shipwreck in Acts 27

Try it out

The account of Paul's shipwreck is a lively piece of narrative near the end of the Acts of the Apostles which offers us a good example to test our understanding of narrative criticism.

Before you go any further, please read Acts 27. (The most fundamental principle of biblical criticism is: first read the passage for yourself!) You might note that it is part of a wider narrative unit that runs on to Acts 28.14, ending, 'And so we came to Rome.'

At first glance this is just a vivid account of a shipwreck. Compare the 44 verses that you have just read with this summary from a Bible atlas:

> The first part of the voyage was via Sidon to Myra in Lycia. There, the party embarked on a wheat ship sailing from Alexandria to Rome. Though late in the season, the captain decided to brave the weather. After passing Crete, the ship was caught by a tempest near the Adriatic Sea and was shipwrecked at Malta. (Aharoni 1968, p. 248)

What we have in Acts 27 is a dramatic, first-person description of a life-changing event. How does narrative criticism help us to see it more clearly?

The events

The story moves quickly towards the drama of the shipwreck. Little space is wasted on the trip from Sidon in verse 3 to Fair Havens in verse 8 (a name which works ironically within the story). Then a note of urgency intervenes – 'much time had been lost' – and danger. The narrative speed slows as Paul advises the centurion to wait. Here is the moment of conflict. The dramatic force of the narrative is heightened when Paul's advice is not followed and the ship heads out to sea, soon to be caught in a violent wind.

For the rest of the chapter the storm rages, vividly described in verses 14–20, 27–30 and 38–43. Between these passages describing the storm and the sailors' struggle to be saved, are two passages in which Paul's voice is heard again. In vv. 21–26 he assures them that they will be saved, despite shipwreck, verse 31 repeats this and in verses 33–37 Paul encourages them to eat for strength, before facing the ordeal of shipwreck. His words recall the fellowship meals of the disciples early in Acts 2.46 and Jesus' last meal with his disciples (Luke 22.19). Verse 43 ends with the whole party safely washed ashore.

The characters

The chief individuals in this narrative are Paul and Julius, the centurion in charge of him. No others are named, though the narrative speaks throughout of 'we' and 'they'. The fact that Julius is named gives his character significance, and his actions affect the drama. He protects and cares for Paul at the start and end of the chapter. In this respect he is Paul's patron. Yet, as a military leader he fails to listen to Paul at a crucial moment in verse 11.

Does this failure matter? This issue raises the theological question of providence. It is relevant to this narrative because, unlike much adventure fiction in the Greco-Roman world, this story claims to describe real events. It could be argued that God would have saved and protected Paul no matter what the centurion decided. But the narrative does not direct its implied readers in this direction. For a start, God never speaks. God is mentioned, but only through Paul, who claims to have seen an angel in the night, and who confesses his faith in God (vv. 23, 25 and 35). The vividness and particularity of the intervening narrative suggests that the centurion's failure to listen to Paul cost everybody dearly.

Paul himself is presented only through direct speech: 'Paul advised them, saying', 'Paul stood up and said', and so on. When the sailors feel safe they do not heed his words but, amid the storm, they receive and obey his guidance. Significantly, Paul does not dwell on the fact that he had been right all along. Instead he leads wisely, respecting the sailors, recognizing and strengthening their courage and giving practical and strategic advice about eating food, before jettisoning their load of grain.

The narrator

The narrator here is clearly identified by the references to 'we' throughout. This feature causes historical critics much trouble, as they seek to account for it, and decide who made up the group, and who the narrator is. The narrative critic is content to note that this use of 'we' is a conventional way one member of a travelling party would describe a journey.

More important is the perspective of this narrator. The narrator begins in verse 1 by noting that decisions about their journey are in the hands of others: 'It was decided.' The narrator is an active observer, noting the progress of the journey from port to port and the changing weather: v. 4 the winds were against us; v. 8 sailing past it with difficulty; v. 9 sailing was now dangerous. The narrator notes the position and suitability of the options for a winter harbour in verse 12: Fair Havens is unsuitable; Phoenix is better. The narrator speaks the language of seafaring throughout the chapter, attending to the details of the sailors' attempts to navigate, with sea anchors, soundings and steering oars. All this presents quite a neutral, descriptive tone. There are no complaints to the captain or centurion, no prayers to God, and no criticism of the sailors, even when they attempt to abandon the ship in the ship's boat. The only glimpse of a personal viewpoint is given in verse 20, when the narrator concedes that in the midst of the tempest 'all our hope of being saved was at last abandoned'.

Paul's calm and reasonable voice is heard all the more clearly then when he speaks, 'Sirs, I can see'; 'Men ... I urge you now.' His last recorded words in this chapter are, 'None of you will lose a hair from your heads', words which echo the words of Jesus according to Luke in 21.18.

Thus, the narrator's perspective is disclosed obliquely here, through the eyes of the unnamed companion(s) of Paul, and in the calm words of Paul. It is a perspective that suggests two things: first that people of faith share the same difficulties as other people, and second that the faith of some offers resources which can benefit all. The indirectness of this perspective makes it seem all the more persuasive – a clever apologetic strategy on the part of the author.

Literary strategies

Apart from the use of direct speech and the careful descriptions of the journey, seafaring and weather, what other literary devices does the narrative employ?

The narrative attends to time and motion throughout. Almost every verse refers to one or both of these matters. Overall, in this journey, Paul is placed outside the normal reference points of space and time. Anthropologists describe this as a liminal setting. The journey shows Paul crossing boundaries, both literally and within himself as a person.

The loss of time mentioned in verse 9 precedes the first pause, when Paul speaks. Here and elsewhere, the narrator slows down the pace of the narrative to build tension. Notably, verses 27–43 describe the events of the end of a single night. Verses 28–29 repeat the process of taking soundings as they drift towards the rocks. Then Paul's voice is heard again, discouraging the sailors from trying to escape in the small boat. At dawn, Paul speaks and acts to encourage and strengthen them, then the ship is lightened and they make a failed attempt to beach the ship. The detail of the narrative at this point is such that the reader feels the immediacy of the howling wind and smashing waves. Time is slowed as the storm rages. Then all motion seems to end as all are finally brought safely to land.

Of course, as with the whole of Acts, there is a link between physical movement and the progress of the gospel. Paul's physical journey and his protection in times of great danger, symbolizes God's protection for the progress of the gospel.

Scholars familiar with the literature of the day point out that this passage draws upon and reflects the popularity of stories about storms and shipwrecks. Such scenes were so common in contemporary travel writing and fiction, that the convention could even be satirized for comic purposes as Lucian (c. 120–180CE) does. Richard Pervo gives the following example to show that the narrative reflects many of the conventional features of a story of a dangerous sea journey:

> Well for a day and a night we sailed before the wind without making very much offing, as land was still dimly in sight; but at sunrise on the second day the wind freshened, the sea rose, darkness came on, and before we knew it, we could no longer get our canvas in. Committing ourselves to the gale and giving up, we drove for seventy-nine days. On the eightieth day, however, the sun came out suddenly and at no great distance we saw a high, wooded island ... (Lucian, *A True Story* 1.6; Pervo 1987, p. 51)

Implied Readers

Finally, who are the implied readers? In the first instance this account appears to be written for those who wished to be entertained, readers of tales of travel and adventure looking for vicarious thrills. They appear not to be Christians, for God is only present through the witness of Paul. As their emotions are roused by the story and by Paul's stirring words within it, they are being encouraged to wish to be like Paul, in his bravery, generosity and faith.

Try it out

This narrative reading of Paul's shipwreck is a rather non-controversial example. You might like to use the same approach with other parts of Luke's narrative that are more central to Christian belief, such as his account of the birth of Jesus in Luke 2.1–20, or his resurrection appearance on the road to Emmaus in Luke 24.13–35.

Consider the events, characters, narrator, literary strategies and implied readers. Even if you don't go through all the steps, take a moment to read through these two passages. What is it about the way they are told that suggests that these and Acts 27 were written/edited by the same person?

Summary of the results of synchronic analysis

After reading this section, the value of the synchronic approach should be clearer. Its main value is in getting us to read the passage observantly for ourselves. The analysis of the structure and shape of the passage, as gained from discourse analysis, enables us to better grasp the whole by seeing it in terms of the relationship of the constituent parts. But close attention to the verbs, the subjects and other key words also helps us identify the content of the passage and the relative importance of different elements.

This prompts us to identify this slogan: 'observation precedes interpretation.' Whenever we interpret a text, it is necessary to pay the closest possible attention to the text itself. No matter how many times we have heard or read a passage before, we need always to guard against careless readings or misreadings.

More radical literary approaches

If linguistic analyses enable us to look at the shape of the passage 'from the outside', literary approaches enable us to look at the passage 'from within'. We consider the flow of the narrative, the viewpoints of its teller and assumed audience, we note who the main characters are, how they are presented and what happens to them. And, using our imaginations, we are able to experience the impact of the narrative for ourselves. We are not so absorbed by it that we lose our own perspective. We do notice how the story achieves its effects, but we make our observations empathetically.

As we have seen, literary interpretations of the text are usually content to allow the text to control what the reader 'sees'. However, there are more radical literary approaches which firmly question this. For example, the flow of a story may reflect a dominant perspective, but the text may incidentally reveal that there are other possible perspectives on the events being presented. Ideological criticism seeks to draw attention to these forbidden or alternative perspectives.

In a more abstract philosophical and linguistic manner deconstruction also challenges the idea that texts have centres that direct how we should understand them. Deconstruction, the most well-known of the poststructuralist approaches to texts, shows that they are in fact incomplete and do not have definite meanings. By reading texts creatively and playfully, it reveals the gaps in their vision and argument. Such strategies are usually adopted to challenge their power over readers. Soulen and Soulen comment, 'The Western longing for meaning based on a stable center is exposed as a kind of bad faith that must make room for the free play of meaning without centers or guarantees' (Soulen and Soulen 2001, p. 45). We will look at ideological approaches to the Bible, including deconstruction, in Chapter 5. Here we just note that such approaches press us to notice that we should not examine the structure or narrative flow of texts naively.

Diachronic approaches

The word 'diachronic' means 'through time'. Diachronic critical tools all look at changes in a text over a period of time: how it was formed, rather than how it is now. These tools should always be used after some synchronic work on the text. Every text deserves to be read carefully and attentively before questions are asked about where it came from and how it came to be the way it is. In practice, it is all too easy to be sidetracked by historical questions and to fail to read the text for ourselves, or to lose confidence in our ability to read it.

Despite the logical force of the argument that we should always begin our interpretation by studying the text synchronically, for much of the twentieth century interpreters began by looking at it historically. No wonder biblical exegesis sometimes has a reputation for being arid. Nevertheless, the books of the Bible are all very old and nearly all of them have a complex history of development. So interpreters do need to consider historical questions such as:

- How did the passage gain its final form?
- What factors influenced its formation?
- What ingredients have been woven into it?
- How has it been edited and with what intentions?

Historical approaches to the text fall logically into three areas. The first looks at how the text developed until it reached its final form. This cluster of methods is known as historical-critical exegesis. The second works towards establishing the most accurate example of this final form by studying the history of its transmission through the manuscripts that survive today. This works towards the reconstruction of the final form and is known as textual criticism. In terms of the history of the text this stage comes later than the first but, because it is necessary to get as close as possible to the final form of the text, interpreters normally begin diachronic analysis with text-critical questions. The third area of historical study considers the impact history of the text. It looks at how it has been received and interpreted through the centuries and all the ways in which these interpretations have affected the world.

Using the original languages

Obviously, the best way of reading a biblical passage is in the original language. This will be classical Hebrew or Aramaic for the Hebrew Bible and *koine* (common) Greek for the New Testament. Hebrew is a member of the Canaanite family of languages, a group of northwest Semitic languages. Most of the Hebrew Bible is written in classical Hebrew, hence its preferred name. From the postexilic period onwards (sixth century BCE), the closely related language of Aramaic replaced Hebrew in public use because it was the administrative language of the Persian empire. Hebrew continued to be used for religious discussion, but various dialects of Aramaic replaced Hebrew in everyday life. The New Testament contains a number of Aramaic words, and it is likely that some dialect of it was Jesus' home language.

Thus, the two languages of the Hebrew Bible are the products of the social and political worlds in which the texts arose. The same is true of the Greek of the New Testament. It is written in a simplified, colloquial Greek dialect called *koine*, which developed through the spread of the empire of Alexander the Great and his successors. The linguistic history of the world in which the Bible arose thus affects our interpretation of it. For example, scholars are still not agreed on whether Jesus spoke only Aramaic, or *koine* Greek as well.

Ideally then, Bible interpretation should be based on the text in Hebrew, Aramaic or Greek. As for all literature, texts in their original languages contain layers of complexity and meaning that are not apparent in translation. Because 'meanings have words' rather than the other way round, there is seldom a direct translation for a word in another language. So, for example, a word in English will have several different translations into Greek, all with slightly different emphases, and a word in Greek may be translated by several different words in English, but none alone will capture the complete meaning of the word. Sometimes biblical writers use subtle word-play to make their point and footnotes to English translations will draw your attention to important instances of this. For example, Amos 8.1–2 records a pun on the similarity of the Hebrew words for 'summer fruit' (*qayits*) and the 'end' (*qets*). Translators may try to reproduce this in English, e.g. by playing on the English words summer and summary execution, but much word-play cannot be reproduced in translation.

Which translation(s) should you use?

If we have not had the opportunity of studying Hebrew, Aramaic or Greek we have no alternative but to study the Bible in translation. The question is, which one? The New Revised Standard Version (1989) is generally regarded as the best English Bible translation to use as a basis for study. There are a number of reasons for this:

- It is the latest revision (hence the words New Revised in the title) in a tradition of translation which goes back to the Authorized Version (1611). Therefore there is a family likeness between this translation and earlier versions such as the American Standard Version (1901) and the Revised Standard Version (New Testament 1946, Hebrew Bible 1952, second edition 1971). Note, that these newer translations make use of advances in textual criticism, and are not just more modern English translations. They are based on more faithful reconstructions of the original Hebrew or Greek texts. See the discussion of textual criticism below.

- Although the work of an American team of translators, it is available in an Anglicized edition, which is suitable for use by native English speakers on this side of the Atlantic.
- It is a scholarly translation, which seeks to be faithful to accepted modern critical editions of the Hebrew Bible and Greek New Testament, without consciously making translation decisions in favour of particular doctrinal positions, as some other translations do at times.
- It also makes moderate use of inclusive language, translating the Greek word for 'brothers' as 'brothers and sisters'. This is not a perfect solution. Sometimes it can be misleading, as when it hides the specifically gendered nature of some biblical argument.

However, those who do not have access to the Bible in the original Hebrew, Aramaic and Greek should never work solely with a single translation when studying the Bible for preaching or teaching. While using the NRSV as a base text, we should compare this translation with other modern translations, both those which aim to be more direct and literal and those which offer a dynamic equivalent paraphrase into contemporary language. The most famous of these is the Good News Bible. One further idea: it is helpful to consult Bible translations into any other modern language that we know. We may well spot new aspects of the text which are not evident in English, such as the distinction between 'you' (singular) and 'you' (plural).

Computers can also help by offering the ability to compare different translations. Some translations are available for quick comparison online at: http://bible.crosswalk.com/ParallelBible.

Textual criticism

Textual criticism has two aims: to reconstruct the original working of the biblical text and to trace the history of transmission of the text (Soulen and

Soulen 2001, p. 189). Neither of these goals can be finally attained, yet the work of textual critics forms the foundation for all Bible translation and interpretation. It offers a disciplined approach for looking closely at how the books of the Bible have been copied and recopied, or provides information about (mostly small) variations between such copies at different times and places. In this way it offers us a unique window into how texts were read (and 'corrected') in earlier periods.

It is the oldest of the historical approaches to the text and in some ways the most difficult. It requires not only a sound knowledge of the biblical languages and other ancient languages into which the Bible was translated, such as Syriac, Coptic, Ethiopic and Old Latin but also a knowledge of associated matters, such as the physical properties of ancient manuscripts, and how scribes and copyists worked.

For these reasons, most biblical interpreters need to rely on the work of specialist scholars. Even interpreters who are able to read the Bible in the original Hebrew or Greek use critical texts which are themselves the fruit of centuries of careful textual criticism. These critical editions offer careful reconstructions of the most likely original forms of the biblical books, with extensive footnotes which indicate where various manuscripts differ from the text they have adopted. Scholars and writers of commentaries working on biblical materials will consider each variation carefully and may arrive at a considered judgement on the text which differs, in places, from the text offered in standard critical editions. These are the *Biblia Hebraica Stuttgartensia*, edited by K. Elliger and W. Rudolph (second edition, 1977) for the Hebrew Bible and the *Novum Testamentum Graece*, edited by E. Nestle, B. and K. Aland, J. Karavidopoulos, C. M. Martini and B. M. Metzger (twenty-seventh edition, 1993). Both of these are periodically updated in the light of ongoing research and are used as the basis of modern biblical translations.

While checking textual variants is an important exegetical step, for everyday interpretation all we need to do is bear in mind that no one today has access to the original copies of the biblical books, and we are all dependent upon the painstaking research of textual critics. They have provided us with texts which are extremely faithful to the earliest existing manuscripts and these texts can be trusted as providing a sound basis for further critical study. Modern translations of the Bible use these modern eclectic reconstructions of the originals. It should be noted that the Authorized Version of the Bible was translated from later and less-reliable manuscripts, so cannot be trusted as an accurate translation for the purposes of historical-critical exegesis.

For practical purposes, when you work on an exegesis from a modern translation like the NRSV you should note any footnotes to your passage. If there are any, these either reflect different possible translations of the original Hebrew, Aramaic or Greek, or variations between different manuscripts. Textual criticism does not deal with translation variations. It is concerned solely with the question of deciding which of the variations between manuscripts is more likely to reflect what was originally written.

If the footnote does identify a variant, usually with the words, 'Other ancient authorities add/omit ...' the textual criticism section of a critical commentary will enable you to consider the pros and cons of such variation(s). You should also try to make up your own mind, using the external and internal criteria which textual critics apply. External criteria concern the age and reliability of the manuscripts. Guides to textual criticism explain which manuscript families are oldest and most reliable. Internal criteria are logical criteria. (For example, because it is likely that difficulties in the text were explained or simplified by later scribes, critics normally consider that the shorter or more difficult reading is likely to be the original one.)

Remember that textual criticism (like all critical work) is an art which is developed through practice and experience. For this reason, interpreters should usually be willing to be guided by the conclusions of the experts. They themselves are usually willing to indicate their degree of certainty about their conclusions, as in the textual commentary edited by B. Metzger, which classifies each judgement listed in the commentary with the letters A, B, C or D, where A indicates certainty, B a high degree of certainty, C doubt about which variant to choose, and D that none of the variants are likely to be original (Metzger 1994, p. 14* – the asterisk relates to the page numbering of the Introduction). Metzger's *Textual Commentary on the Greek New Testament* provides enough information for most everyday exegesis of the New Testament. There is no similar reference work for the whole of the Hebrew Bible, but critical commentaries provide full discussions of text-critical matters and there are guides to textual criticism of the Hebrew Bible (e.g. Brotzman 1994) and guides to using the *Biblica Hebraica* (e.g. Wonneberger 1990).

Try it out

Look at the text of the Lord's Prayer recorded in Luke 11.2–4. Now look at the footnotes to the NRSV, and identify which notes refer to text variants and which suggest different translations. Where the differences are between manuscripts, the longer version of the Lord's Prayer found in Matthew's Gospel (Matt. 6.9–13) was, and still is, more widely known. The text-critical guideline of preferring the shorter reading means that this text does not include the longer variant readings of some manuscripts.

Incidentally, this example helps us see the point of all historical criticism, which starts with textual criticism. We need the tools of historical criticism to answer important questions like: If the Gospels record two versions of the Lord's Prayer, which is closest to the prayer Jesus taught? By what processes, and for what reasons, did the Gospels of Matthew and Luke develop these two different versions of that original prayer?

The history of the language being used

In our discussion of discourse analysis above, we found that by paying close attention to the text we were able to identify key words. In Genesis 11.1–9 these were verbs like 'migration' and 'settlement', 'brick-making' and 'building', 'scattering' and 'confusion' and subjects like 'the whole earth', 'they', 'the Lord' and 'the city'. Another key word was 'language'.

A historical approach now asks: What if anything do we need to find out about the history of these words or word patterns to deepen our understanding of the passage? To think historically about them, we have to think of the words in the original Hebrew. If we cannot read Hebrew, we need to draw on the expertise and findings of those who do. There are many treasures to be discovered in commentaries and studies, old and new. But, as with all quests for hidden treasure, there are dangers too. If we turn to commentaries too soon, we may be overwhelmed or distracted by the volume of technical information, or discouraged by finding that the commentators are not answering the questions we have.

If we are able to read Hebrew or Greek, or at least know enough to use theological dictionaries and lexicons, we should look up the key words in the passage. This is to ensure that we are sensitive to the particular meanings that are, and are not, likely to be represented by them. For example, what is the significance of the pun on the Hebrew word for 'confuse' (*balal*) in Genesis 11.9 and the name of the tower (Babel)? To take a New Testament example also beginning with 'b', the meaning of the Greek word translated 'barbarians' in Romans 1.14 does not have the same negative meaning as in modern English. Paul simply uses it as a common expression for non-Greeks, which mimics how a foreign language sounded to Greeks: 'bar-bar'.

Interpreters need to be meticulous about locating the meaning of words historically. It is not responsible to review all the possible meanings of a word and then to translate it with the one meaning that most closely suits our purpose. We need to think historically about what the word was likely to mean and imply at the time it was originally used. If the text has a long history of development, we will also need to consider possible shifts in the meaning of the word at the various stages in the formation of the text. For example, an older text may have been woven into a later one, or edited to serve a new purpose.

Try it out

Make a note to yourself to see how commentators either are or are not sensitive to thinking historically about the meanings of words and ideas in the Genesis 11.1–9.

For example, do they consider 'making a name for oneself' to be a good or a bad thing? Does this phrase mean that the people in the narrative wanted to be remembered (that is not completely forgotten) or famous (better remembered than others)? There is no simple answer to this question, yet it is necessary to make a decision about this in order to offer an interpretation of that passage.

Form criticism

We have already seen that in order to read a passage sensibly we have to make a preliminary judgement about what kind of literature it is. That is, its genre. Broadly speaking this means registering the obvious: whether our passage is a historical narrative, a parable, an apocalypse, a Gospel, a letter, or whatever. Such a general identification is essential for any literary approach to the passage as it is now.

It is also essential to thinking historically about the passage. For example, people don't write Gospels or apocalypses today, so we have to think historically about the common features of these genres for those who wrote in them. What conventions governed their construction and interpretation at the time they were originally written and read, or spoken and heard? However, even a genre as familiar as a letter needs to be thought of historically, because the conventions governing the structure and contents of letters were different in the hellenistic world of the first century CE.

So, determining the genre of a passage is part of form criticism. However, as it has developed as a critical method since the early years of the twentieth century, it goes beyond this. It poses two particular historical questions of biblical texts:

- Is there evidence that all or part of the passage first existed in an oral form before being included within this written document?
- If so, in what sort of life situation (*Sitz im Leben* is the technical German term) might it have been used?

In trying to answer these two questions, form criticism builds on the answers already offered by synchronic readings of the text about its structure, shape and genre. Often an analysis of the structure reveals elements which suggest their earlier use elsewhere, whether in oral or written form, such as proverbs or hymns. Other examples of preliterary forms or patterns include: laments, parables, proverbs, laws, tales, myths, legends, call stories, beatitudes, healing stories, nature miracles, resurrection accounts, creeds, slogans, blessings and curses.

In this brief outline of form criticism, we come up against an issue which recurs throughout this book: Should methods of interpretation developed at particular times for particular purposes continue to be used in changed circumstances? We ask this because methods of interpretation are naturally affected by the spirit of the age in which they arise. Form criticism rightly reminds us to consider the relationships between the genre, the shape and the function of units of tradition, particularly units of tradition which appear to have been shaped by oral usage. However, older examples of form criticism of the New Testament were unduly limiting when they assumed that units of oral tradition mainly arose in worship situations ('cultic occasions'), such as baptisms, the eucharist and sermons (Berger in Hayes 1999, p. 414). Older examples of form criticism have also been accused of 'historical scepticism and sociological determinism' by assuming that communities adapted and even generated tradition to suit their immediate needs (Muddiman in Coggins and Houlden 1990, p. 242).

Clearly we should not assume a simple, direct relationship between the forms of units of oral tradition and their origins and purposes. Yet, such objections should not prevent us from using form critical questions to gain insights about the oral basis of much of the Bible. It does contain oral traditions which were both as fixed and as influential upon the faith of the first readers and writers as popular hymns are upon people today.

To use form criticism as a tool, we need to cover the following four steps:

- First, decide where the unit we are studying begins and ends and how it is structured. We need to be able to explain our analysis of the structure, as we did in our synchronic analyses of part of Genesis 11 and Acts 27.
- Second, determine the genre, or genres used in the text. Historical commentaries will often refer to other examples of such genres within the Bible or other texts from a similar period.
- Third, consider the literary, historical and social settings of the text. That is, where it fits within the book of the Bible it comes from, what stage of the history of Israel or early Christianity it belongs to, and what social context(s) it relates to.
- Finally, decide how this information helps us think about what these earlier units of oral tradition were originally for.

Try it out

Try out the four steps above by reading Deuteronomy 26 and identifying the earlier confession of faith incorporated in it. A further example of a creed incorporated within Deuteronomy is the Shema in Deuteronomy 6.4–9.

How does your identification of this earlier oral tradition affect your reading of this chapter? Consider why the prophets and priest who assembled Deuteronomy might have wished to include this creed here.

Source criticism

All we have said about the importance of thinking about genre, shape and function is relevant to source criticism too. As the oldest of the historical critical tools (excluding textual criticism), it has a long and particular history of development. However, like form criticism, it also raises a simple and crucial question about the composition of a passage: Does it incorporate any pre-existing sources? While form criticism looks for evidence of oral sources, source criticism looks for evidence of written sources. If it finds evidence of these, it seeks to classify them according to genre, and ask where they come from, what their perspective is, and why the author has incorporated them within the passage under consideration.

The crucial consequence of finding evidence of a written source is that it often has a different character from the passage in which it is now embedded. It may, for example, have a different view of God, or embody a different ethical principle. The next question that arises is: Why would authors incorporate a passage expressing views that differ from their own? There are various reasons for this. They may wish to show their awareness of other views, or show their respect for older traditions, in order to gain the sympathy of their readers. Whatever the reason for this, when authors create texts from other sources they raise questions in the minds of readers about what the author's own perspectives are.

Well-known examples of multiple source usage in the Bible are the Pentateuch, in which a number of sources have been detected, and the Gospels of Matthew and Luke, which each appear to use Mark's Gospel, together with another written source, known as Q, and possible written sources of their own, tagged M and L for short. This data alone shows that source criticism is an important tool for biblical interpretation. This also creates problems for those who wish to interpret the Bible literally. For example, which of the two creation narratives in Genesis 1–2 describes how God actually created the world? For that matter, did Noah take two pairs (Gen. 6.20) or seven pairs (Gen. 7.3) of every kind of bird into the ark?

Try it out

Using a Gospel parallels book or the online resources at http://www.utoronto.ca/religion/synopsis/ or http://www.bible-researcher.com/parallels.html compare Jesus' teaching on divorce in Matt. 5.31–32 and in Luke 16.18. These passages have some common features that suggest they come from a common source.

First, note the common features (and that a related passage in Matt. 19.19 relates better to Mark 10.11–12) and judge for yourself whether these do imply their use of a common source.

Then, consider the very different use made of this material in Matthew and Luke. What does this tell you about their different concerns and emphases? For example, why does Luke tuck away this unit of tradition amid a large section on the use of riches, while Matthew embeds it within teaching on anger, lust and oaths? In Matthew's mind, is looking at a woman lustfully, the same kind of adultery as marrying a divorced woman? In Luke's mind, is the abuse of riches far more important than the question of divorce and adultery? This question of the theological interests of the different Gospel writers is dealt with further by redaction criticism (see below).

Finally, notice how this historical thinking makes it clear that it is not easy to say 'what Jesus actually taught' on this topic.

Similarly, notice the way source-critical analysis distances you from feeling the persuasive force of each narrative. Does this matter?

Tradition criticism

A further spin on the question of how texts use traditional material is considered by tradition criticism. Traditions are relatively fixed, yet they also change and develop over time. For example, consider how patterns of shared family meals have changed in the last generation.

Tradition criticism traces the change and development in traditions over the period before they become incorporated into the passage under consideration. As a method it developed out of the efforts of form critics of the Hebrew Bible to reconstruct the stages of development of a text from its earliest oral stages to its final written form. These scholars thought the Pentateuch evolved out of cycles of oral tradition. Hebrew Bible scholars have tended to use tradition history as an overarching method to trace all the developing stages of the text from early parallels in other cultures and religions to the place of the tradition within the biblical canon.

Gnuse (in Hayes 1999, vol. 2, p. 586) applies the five stages of tradition history analysis to the well-known story of the call of the boy Samuel in 1 Samuel 3. He shows how this story can be fitted into wider and wider cycles of tradition or narrative. To get the most from his example, please read the Bible passage first.

- Analysis of comparable prophetic narratives and dream reports from other literature of the ancient near east offers examples of similar experiences, especially night-time prophetic dream reports at shrines in Mari (1800 BCE) and 'auditory message dreams' from Egypt and Mesopotamia.

- Form criticism of the passage indicates that verses 1–18 contain the original form of the text and identifies literary devices in the plot development (e.g. contrast between the aged Eli and the young Samuel, and the three-fold call pattern which heightens suspense). Similarities between this and other call narratives in the Hebrew Bible (such as Moses in Exodus 3 or Saul in 1 Samuel 9) are noted.

- 1 Samuel 3 is then located within the wider context of 1 Samuel 1–3. This larger narrative cycle compares the young Samuel with the evil priests of the time and has common themes with the Elohist cycle in the Pentateuch which also has auditory message dreams, a positive view of prophets and a distrust of priests.

- The larger unit of tradition of 1 Samuel 3 is then located within a wider narrative cycle about the rise of the monarchy in 1 Samuel 1–15. This further supports the view that prophets are better than kings, a view which seems to come from the final deuteronomic editors. (This step resembles redaction criticism, see below.) In this way, 1 Samuel 3 can be seen to play an important role in stressing the authority of the prophetic word.

- The whole deuteronomic history can then be related to the theological themes of the entire Hebrew Bible and the contribution of 1 Samuel 3 can be related to them. (This is canonical criticism, which we look at in Chapter 5 below.)

New Testament scholars recognize the importance of tracing lines of development within important New Testament traditions, for example, in the words of institution that Paul passes on regarding the Lord's Supper.

Try it out

Compare the forms of wording of Jesus' institution of the Lord's Supper in Mark 14.22–25 and 1 Cor. 11.23–26 in the table below.

What are the differences between them and how would you account for them? 1 Corinthians was written in 56–7 CE and Mark about ten to fifteen years later. Can we talk about the development of this tradition over such a short time, or are the differences between these two uses of the tradition more determined by the theological purposes of the two writers?

1 Corinthians 11.23–26	Mark 14.22–25
23 For I received from the Lord what I also handed on to you, that the Lord Jesus on the night when he was betrayed took a loaf of bread, 24 and when he had given thanks, he broke it and said, 'This is my body that is for you. Do this in remembrance of me.' 25 In the same way he took the cup also, after supper, saying, 'This cup is the new covenant in my blood. Do this, as often as you drink it, in remembrance of me.' 26 For as often as you eat this bread and drink the cup, you proclaim the Lord's death until he comes.	22 While they were eating, he took a loaf of bread, and after blessing it he broke it, gave it to them, and said, 'Take; this is my body.' 23 Then he took a cup, and after giving thanks he gave it to them, and all of them drank from it. 24 He said to them, 'This is my blood of the covenant, which is poured out for many. 25 Truly I tell you, I will never again drink of the fruit of the vine until that day when I drink it new in the kingdom of God.'

Redaction criticism

The final stage in the historical development of a text is the revision work done on it by a later editor or reviser. Redaction criticism was a reaction to the tendency of form criticism to fragment biblical texts into small units. It attempts to redress the balance by considering the whole picture, looking particularly for evidence of the perspective of the final author or editor in the way the work has been shaped and assembled.

Redaction criticism can only be used when there are identifiable sources, such as can be found in Deuteronomy or Acts. For this reason it is a particularly important tool for the study of the synoptic Gospels (Matthew, Mark and Luke). Where such sources are known, redaction critics can compare the text under examination with the sources to see how the writer/editor has adapted these sources and with what purpose. By considering the additions and changes made by the final writer(s) or editor(s) redaction criticism is able to identify the theological emphases and convictions of those responsible for shaping the final form of the text.

Try it out

Compare the two passages from Mark 6 and Luke 9 below with two redactional critical questions in mind. First, note what changes Luke makes to the Marcan tradition which identifies John the Baptist with Elijah. Next, try to suggest why Luke might have made these changes (Soulen and Soulen 2001, p. 159).

Notice that redaction criticism works with little clues or hints. Here it probes the text for hints of what Mark and Luke respectively thought of Herod, or what the people believed about the resurrection of the beheaded John, and in what respects they thought that Herod (or the people) thought that John (or Jesus) was the new Elijah.

What this process reveals is that Luke's view of how Jesus' ministry is related to that of the line of prophets is different from that of Mark.

Mark 6	Luke 9
14 King Herod heard of it, for Jesus' name had become known. Some were saying, 'John the baptizer has been raised from the dead; and for this reason these powers are at work in him.' *15* But others said, 'It is Elijah.' And others said, 'It is a prophet, like one of the prophets of old.' *16* But when Herod heard of it, he said, 'John, whom I beheaded, has been raised.' *17* For Herod himself had sent men who arrested John, bound him, and put him in prison on account of Herodias, his brother Philip's wife, because Herod had married her.	*7* Now Herod the ruler heard about all that had taken place, and he was perplexed, because it was said by some that John had been raised from the dead, *8* by some that Elijah had appeared, and by others that one of the ancient prophets had arisen. *9* Herod said, 'John I beheaded; but who is this about whom I hear such things?' And he tried to see him.

Background information

This concludes the range of diachronic critical methods which are normally termed 'historical-critical'. However, there is also a wide range of information which interpreters need to assemble if they are to apply these methods in an informed way. Often a circular approach has to be adopted here, that is to say the interpreter begins by tentatively locating the formation period of the text and then adjusts this in the light of information yielded by historical-critical research. This is true for work on all texts in all genres.

For all texts that claim to describe historical events, other dates have to be considered, such as:

• When did the events described actually take place?
• What are the dates of the various stages of the passage's formation? For example, dates when the oral cycle was formed, dates of written sources, dates of various stages of editing.

The latter dates will help the interpreter to consider in what ways the passage may be addressing issues relating to stages of its formation or editing, rather than the time it describes.

For a passage with a long development history, the historical interpreter will need to consider the relevant background information for all these periods. While a wide range of reference books can be consulted, as well as the growing quantity of information accessible on the internet, standard reference works on biblical backgrounds should be the first port of call. For the Hebrew Bible see A. S. van der Woude's *The World of the Bible* (1986) or the revised and expanded edition of John Rogerson and Philip Davies' *The Old Testament* World (2005). For New Testament studies, the best single volume is Everett Ferguson's *Backgrounds of Early Christianity* (third edition, 2003). A much fuller and recent (but expensive) publication is the two-volume *The Biblical World*, edited by John Barton (2002).

Such general volumes need to be supplemented by books on Israelite history, and the history of the world in the hellenistic era for the intertestamental and New Testament period, the geography of the ancient near east and books on the social, economic, political, cultural and religious world of the ancient near east. For this purpose a bibliographic guide is helpful. The most comprehensive and up to date is *An Annotated Guide to Biblical Resources for Ministry* by David Bauer (2003).

When it comes to specific passages, we often need to refer to more specialist reference materials. For example, for Acts 27 we need to know not only about the geography and archaeology of the relevant places in the Mediterranean, and first-century seafaring practices, but even about the conventions of the hellenistic novel. The Greek novel *Chaereas and Callirhoe*, written roughly at the same time as Acts, gives us a good idea about sea travel in the first century. Such primary sources also give modern readers a helpful window into the popular mind of the first century CE. To take another example, a letter written towards the end of the novel has echoes of Paul's letter to Philemon (see Reardon 1989, p. 116).

Impact history

So far, we have looked at tools for reading a passage in its final form and tools for tracing the history of its formation. Though it is also a historical discipline, textual criticism serves both of these approaches because it is the tool we rely on to provide us with a copy of each book of the Bible which is closest to what the original authors wrote.

Before we leave diachronic approaches, however, there is one further aspect of the history of the text we need to note. That is to ask what effect it has had on people down the centuries since it was written. All great works of art and literature have such an impact history, which is more than a history of interpretation. Think, for example, of the difference between musicological study of the roots of Elvis Presley's new brand of rock and roll, and the effect that his music and the rock and roll it gave birth to has had on the world since the 1950s.

The critical tools we have used so far have produced a variety of results, but they have tended to keep the text at a distance. Discourse analysis and literary criticism are both rather analytical, though they can give us the satisfaction of feeling that we are reading the text attentively. The historical-critical approaches all look 'behind' the text for information about the text, rather than allowing the text to tell speak for itself. While recognizing the value of this historical information, many Bible interpreters today have become dissatisfied with this distancing effect. There has been a shift of interest away from looking behind the text to looking 'in front' of it: to what the Bible has meant and said to people down the centuries. In Chapter 5 we take this process further by looking at the methods contemporary readers use to let them hear the message of the Bible for themselves.

While it may appear as if those who study and teach the Bible professionally in colleges or universities are quite content with literary and historical approaches to the Bible, in fact there are many who recognize that the discipline needs to relate its work more closely to the concerns and questions of 'real life'. One of the ways biblical scholars have begun to reconnect the Bible with the world 'out there' is through the study of the impact history of the Bible.

Impact history (sometimes known by the German term *Wirkungsgeschichte*) is more than just studying the history of biblical interpretation. It is the study of all the different ways in which each passage of the Bible has been received and has exercised an influence upon human life. As such, it is clearly a way of looking at the Bible, rather than a method for interpreting it. It reminds us of the enormous scope of the Bible's influence upon the world and the way in which all sorts of people, known and unknown, have contributed to this process through the centuries. Precisely because of its breadth, impact history has the capacity to draw in a wide range of data that is normally excluded by other approaches to biblical interpretation. One way of handling this quantity of material is by focusing on a particular strand of impact history. For example, Christopher Rowland's work on the book of Revelation (1998, with Kovacs 2004, and 2005) pays close attention to its impact on western art.

Markus Bockmuehl, a leading New Testament scholar from Cambridge University, writes that impact history is one of the few contemporary approaches to the New Testament that is able to integrate the academic study of the New Testament and prevent it from 'going down the plughole' (1998, pp. 295–8)! Similarly, the Swiss scholar Ulrich Luz includes a major focus on impact history (sometimes also called the 'history of effects') in his commentary on Matthew's Gospel to show that social and political circumstances have always affected how the Bible is interpreted and that these interpretations in turn affect the course of history.

By looking at the ways in which the Bible has affected all aspects of human history, impact history takes a firmly historical approach to the Bible. It expects us to have paid close attention to the final form of the text and also to have taken account of the history of its formation. But its main purpose is to invite us to dive into the vast subject of how the text has been used and received over many centuries; and this is where things become interesting. Impact history shows us that interpreters frequently do not prefer the plain meaning of the text, and it asks us to consider why this should be. By making us face the fact that all biblical texts have had a wide variety of interpretations through history, it supports the postmodern view that texts have many possible meanings. At the same time, it moderates this view, by also showing that there are limits to the range of meanings of each text. Texts can be interpreted in more than one way, but they also robustly resist being assigned arbitrary or alien meanings. Impact history shows both that differing circumstances reveal different aspects of the range of meaning within a text, and that some attempts to assign meanings beyond this range have been later shown later to be irresponsible and illegitimate.

As a perspective on the Bible, impact history is also helpful in moving us back to the question of why we are interpreting a passage. Seeing the range of possible meanings that a passage has had over its history, we are forced to make a decision about which interpretation we prefer, at least for here and now. But, noticing the effects that good or bad interpretations have had on human life they also require us to consider the implications of our preferred interpretation for the world or the church. They require us to take responsibility for the consequences of our interpretations. We cannot claim to be merely disinterested scholars.

Impact history works with four hermeneutical principles:

- the context of the interpreter is important;
- interpretations in turn affect the context in which they are made;
- human history, the history of the text and the text itself are all valued;
- interpreters often adopt interpretations which cannot be defended on historical-critical grounds.

Overall, it gives abundant proof that the meanings of texts are profoundly affected by the identity and purposes of those using them.

Try it out:

The Internet is a good place to get an initial impression of the range of effects of a biblical passage. To test this out, insert 'the good Samaritan' (with inverted commas) into a search engine like Google. The UK Google website can be found at http://www.google.co.uk. Now review your results.

This is the sort of information that you may discover:

- It is the name of many caring institutions: hospitals, churches, crisis centres and service organizations in the USA and Canada, usually with a Christian foundation.
- It is a byword for 'effective compassion'.
- The American Bible Society have prepared a major 'new media' study resource on this parable.
- People write new plays and poems about the parable.
- There are links to many paintings representing this parable: for example, a painting by Hogarth (1737) hanging in St Bartholomew's Hospital, London.
- It is the basis of a number of urban legends, following a similar format in which a mechanic helps someone whose car has broken down as an act of kindness. Having reluctantly given the person his name and address, he learns later that the person in distress was very rich (Donald Trump or Bill Gates) and he receives a large reward.

This story also has had a huge impact on art. To see this, perform a similar search for images (this time click on the Images tab at the top of the page).

There are some common features associated with the impact history of the phrase 'the good Samaritan'. The main effect of this parable seems to have been to inspire acts of compassion and care. While detailed research into the precise social location of Samaritans in first-century Israel may yield interesting results for interpreters, the key question by which these results should be evaluated is: Do they intensify or help to focus or direct this important effect? For example, it should be able to explain that distinterested compassion is a core value of the parable and in this respect the urban legends fundamentally misunderstand it.

Whether we try this out with a well-known or little-known passage, we may be surprised to notice that many older Bible commentaries pay almost no attention to impact history. This situation is changing however. As already mentioned, Ulrich Luz's major commentary on Matthew's Gospel devotes a great deal of attention to this topic, and the Blackwell Bible Commentary series is now focused entirely on this approach. The website contains much useful material in which the authors reflect on the scope of their projects. See: http://www.bbibcomm.net/index.html for the home page which provides links to how different commentators are approaching their tasks. Not surprisingly, there are some difficulties with this approach. The main ones are:

- How to select and order the vast amounts of disparate material.
- How to evaluate interpretations.
- Whether to include interpretations that are clearly wrong or immoral (e.g. the many anti-Jewish statements found in biblical interpretations of late antiquity and the medieval periods).
- And how to ensure that each commentary is more than just a catalogue of effects and actually sheds light on the biblical text.

Despite such problems, these writers are aware of the richness of the field for study. Many of the contributors report that they find it deeply satisfying to be exploring the moments of performance or impact when biblical passages meet the world.

Try it out

You might like to visit the Centre for Reception History of the Bible to follow how a group of scholars are exploring this area. See http://www.crhb.org/index.html

Or, you might like to investigate the impact history of another Bible passage for yourself. Remember that impact history is not a method or tool, but an approach to the Bible. It invites us to come to it with more of ourselves. Ulrich Luz says, 'the understanding of a biblical text happens not only through the elucidation of its statements but beyond that by practising and suffering, by singing and poetry, by praying and hoping' (Luz 1989, p. 98).

Choose a Bible passage that relates to a topic that interests you and begin to investigate links between this passage and your interest area. You will almost certainly discover that others have done this before you and that you find their views deeply enriching, interesting or downright annoying. This may well lead you to look more deeply into why others hold the views they do, and why some of these views are so different from yours.

Again, the Internet provides a useful starting point for your investigation. For example, if you, like one of the authors mentioned have an interest in the parable of the prodigal son and in dancing, you might insert the following into a search engine: 'music and dancing' + Bible.

The impact history of the Bible reminds us that biblical interpretation is a relational task in that it is done by, with and for others. Ulrich Luz argues that our interpretations should 'help others to experience joy, freedom and identity' and also help them 'in their external needs, in their hunger and sufferings' (Luz 1994, p. 94). To help us do this the next chapter offers ways of looking more closely at ourselves and others.

4

Our Reality

The role of the reader

The importance of the reader in biblical interpretation has become more widely recognized in recent decades. Biblical scholars have begun to take note of who is doing the reading as well as what is being read. In line with scholars such as Michel Foucault (1926–84) this Studyguide suggests texts are works in process, rather than fixed by their original author. Thus the meaning of the text depends on the reader as well as the writer.

Reader-response criticism

As we noted in Chapter 2, the Bible is dependent on people to open, read and respond to it. Reader-response criticism is interested in the process of reading and recognizes the work the reader has to do to make sense of the text. The meaning of the text emerges through reading and is therefore reliant on the reader as well as the text. These methods regard the reading of the text as a performance in which the reader has a vital role to play, from making literal sense of the text to supplying gaps in the narrative and ironing out repetition (Gillingham 1998, p. 183).

Readers' expectations and life experiences guide their reading of a text in many ways. They may linger with one aspect of the story more than another or make a moral judgement based on their own value system. Gina Hens-Piazza notes also the role of the reader in character formation, describing the text version as 'only an initial draft' (Hens-Piazza 2003, p. 11) from which the reader builds up a fuller picture. She suggests this process happens more often with minor characters who have only a few lines in a story since there is more scope for the reader's imagination. The reader reads ideas and associations into the story to flesh out such characters. However, they cannot be moulded into any shape the reader chooses since the text also sets proper limits to his/her interpretation (Hens-Piazza 2003, pp. 12–13).

Soulen and Soulen note a divergence of opinion among reader response critics as to whether the text is free to be interpreted without constraint, or whether it had a privileged meaning for its original audience that readers today should seek to locate (Soulen and Soulen 2001, p. 157). Total interpretative freedom removes any safeguards and raises the question of whether there remain any accepted grounds for contesting inaccurate or miscreant readings.

Try it out

Read 1 Corinthians 12.14–31. How would you test the validity of new or divergent readings of this passage? Are there any boundaries to interpretation and if so, what are they?

The obvious implication of reader-response theory is that each new reader responds to the text differently, creating the possibility that a biblical passage has more than one meaning.

The realities of life inform all our reading – even at the basic level of whether we are able to read it. UN sources note that there are still approximately one billion illiterate adults in the world today (figure cited in UN press release on International Literacy Day 2001). Chinese women, returning to their rural communities from a Bible conference remind each other:

> We are going home to many who cannot read
> so, Lord, make us to be Bibles,
> so that those who cannot read the book
> can read it in us. (Anonymous, in Katusno-Ishii and Orteza 2000, p. 87)

Acknowledging our historical and social location is vital if we are to read the Bible responsibly. This chapter, therefore, is about asking the necessary questions of ourselves as we stand before the text, recognizing how:

> different readers, shaped in diverse ways by the interaction of such variables as religious tradition, gender, national origin, race and ethnicity, socio-economic class, political affiliation and a host of comparable social factors, attribute multiple and even contradictory meanings to the 'same' biblical texts. (Stone 2002, p. 78)

Try it out

Think of a recent film you have seen and discussed with other people. How did your interpretation of the film differ from theirs? Consider how your own life experience influences your interpretation of films.

Reading for ourselves

Tiffany and Ringe (1996, p. 25) encourage us to begin our journey with the Bible 'at home', paying attention to our own situation first. What are the defining characteristics that give us our unique shape? How do we identify ourselves when others ask us, 'Who are you?' There are so many different elements to our identity; some we are comfortable talking about, and others we hide.

Try it out

Begin by listing, in no particular order, the different ways you describe yourself. You can include anything you like – serious or silly, something quite unusual or something you share with millions of others. This is just a quick identity sketch that only you need to see. Once you have spent a few minutes on this, read through your list and see if there is anything that surprises you. Have you forgotten anything important?

One of the authors made the following identity sketch:

> I am a feminist; a Wolves fan; of white ethnic identity which awards me unearned privileges in life; I'm still listening to Radio 1; a vegan; my theological perspective is most influenced by Latin American liberation theology; I wear glasses.

Not all of these characteristics will have equal bearing on her reading of the Bible, but all shape her perspective in some way or another. She will be able to see some things in the texts more clearly because of her identity and experience (provided she's wearing her glasses!) and other aspects of a passage will remain hidden or irrelevant to her.

Randy Litchfield points out that our identity provokes both contact and distance between people since:

> identity forms at the boundaries and intersections of social locations as much as at their centers ... Individuals uniquely embody the intersections of many social locations. Thus, difference amongst individuals is a given. Yet people *do* share particular social locations with others, which suggests commonalities. (Litchfield 2004, pp. 232–3)

Some aspects of our identity are more likely to create wider connections with others (e.g. our gender), while other more unusual qualities mark us out as different, until we encounter others who share those specific marks of identification (e.g. left-handed people).

There are three more things to note about this self-identification process: we identify ourselves differently depending on where we are, who we are with and for what purpose we are being asked; we can never fully describe ourselves (and similarly, we can never adequately sum up the reality of another person); we are always all, and more than, our defining characteristics.

We have multiple and fluid identities that develop through time and experience. To illustrate this, Robert Beckford draws parallels between identity formation of young people in New York City and the technical layering of sounds within hip hop. Sounds are built up to create a new track, just as young people deconstruct and mix up traditions and cultures to form new identities (Beckford 2001, p. 106).

In this chapter we focus on five key aspects of our identity that have been recognized as affecting on our interpretation of the Bible in recent years: gender and sexuality; ethnicity; age, ability and well-being; socio-economic status and political affiliation; and denominational, spiritual and theological traditions.

Despite the multifaceted nature of our identity, any one person is only able to read from one place at a time. While the particularity of any reading is difficult to deny, western biblical scholars who were usually white and male, seldom acknowledged the restricted nature of their readings until liberationist movements, through naming their own location, forced them to recognize their specific identity. Even then, some theologians failed to fully acknowledge their particularity. For example, early feminist theology was based on the experience of middle-class white women and it was only through painful dialogue with black and Asian women that this was properly acknowledged. Soulen and Soulen note how readers who explicitly identify their location believe they are less vulnerable to ideological distortions (Soulen and Soulen 2001, p. 1).

Many first-world theologians now also recognize the importance of naming their location. One example would be Eleanor Haney, a theologian living and working with church communities in Maine, the vast east coast state. She locates herself in the following way:

> I am white, of northern European ancestry and culture, female, academically trained with a PhD, in a lesbian relationship, a member of a largely white and middle-class Protestant denomination, from a lower-middle-class background, sixty-five years old, representative of the culture's understanding of mental and emotional normalcy, physically able-bodied, and an easterner who deeply loves the ocean. (Haney 1998, p. 6)

Moreover, she notes, 'As a white middle-class Christian feminist, I can only do white middle-class Christian feminist theology and ethics. My experience and perspectives, though limited, can nevertheless contribute to a larger, rainbow-hued understanding of justice, theology and ethics' (Haney 1998, p. 1).

Haney recognizes the demands her location places on her theology and the authority that comes from an authenticity of place. In locating the particularity of her interpretation, she enables her contribution to be an honest part of the dialogue between people of different locations.

We turn now to a closer examination of each of the five areas of identity listed above. It is artificial to treat each characteristic separately, since we retain all these aspects of our identity at all times. However, for clarity, we will focus on one element at a time.

Gender and sexuality

Try it out

At the beginning of each of these five sections, you are encouraged to reflect on some aspect of your identity. For this section, you will find it helpful to note down a description of your gender and sexuality. How do you feel about this aspect of your identity? How do you think it might affect your reading of the Bible?

We cannot read the Bible as non-specific human beings, but only as gendered persons. This does not prevent our interpretations from providing insights that cross gender boundaries, for example, both men and women can relate to a passage that describes hunger or friendship or joy – although there will no doubt be nuanced understandings of even such a basic human experience as hunger (for example, a man might consider hunger through the traditional lens of needing to be the 'breadwinner' and a woman might reflect on traditional female roles of cooking food and providing nourishment).

While aware of the danger of rehearsing gender stereotypes, the following paragraphs describe some of the ways in which gender and sexual orientation may affect biblical interpretation.

There may be blind spots in our reading due to our gendered experience of life. For example, women readers would be better able to understand the experience of the women with the haemorrhages (Mark 5), and men may be more able to relate to the discussion concerning male circumcision in Galatians. Women and men also tend to identify, at least initially, with different biblical characters or situations. Moreover, the church has perpetuated certain gendered identifications, for example, of women with Mary. In response, feminist theologians have accused the church of offering women an impossible role model – that of the virgin mother.

Dominant interpretations of the Bible restrict roles for men and women. Furthermore, texts such as the household codes (Col. 3.18–4.1; Eph. 5.22–6.9; 1 Pet. 2.13–3.7) have been used to prescribe a hierarchical model of gender relationships. Readers may need to search out alternative role models, even crossing gender lines to discover new ways of being. Jesus certainly modelled a radically different way of being male.

Women and homosexual people often have to imagine themselves into the biblical text. This has led to a greater alertness to minor characters caught in the shadows of the story. One example of this is the reclaiming of Hagar (Gen. 19–21) as a central biblical character within womanist theology. Another example is the work of queer interpreters (the description chosen by many gay, lesbian, bisexual and transgender readers) in recalling the likely presence of queer people in many events described in the Bible, even if the text fails to mention them. Queer readers have also noted visible sexual outcasts in the Bible such as eunuchs, Nehemiah being one example. Goss and West note the need to be, 'resistant readers who struggle against heterocentric privilege that erases us from the text. As queer readers, we want to befriend the Scriptures to find our voices and allow subversive memories and diversities to emerge' (Goss and West 2000, p. 6).

Those who have experienced the Bible as oppressive or excluding read the Bible with less expectation of liberation. These groups are more willing to challenge traditional readings of texts, for example feminist interpreters have questioned the portrayal of Delilah as a seductive temptress and reconsidered the heroic standing of Samson within the story (Judg. 16).

Through these observations, can we conclude that women and men read the Bible differently? It is important to note that not all women identify as feminists. Moreover, some men are committed to feminist practice, for example, hymnwriter Brian Wren whose book, *What Language Shall I Borrow? God-talk in Worship: A Male Response to Feminist Theology* tries to develop a positive male theology. With such qualifications in mind, when we look at feminist and womanist biblical interpretation we can nevertheless identify certain defining characteristics that have emerged since women became more vocal in academic biblical interpretation.

Feminist and womanist interpretation is often marked by:

- collaboration with other interpreters;
- giving priority to women's experience, even over the biblical text;
- a greater awareness of the silences within the text and the marginal characters of a story;
- an unwillingness to condemn acts of survival that do not fit the established morality;
- a commitment to exposing violence within a text or interpretation of a text;
- a willingness to deny the validity of a text if it is experienced as oppressive;
- greater willingness to accept syncretism within the text and within interpretative methods through the use of non-biblical sources to critique the text. (An example of this tendency is Chung Hyun Kyung's speech at the World Council of Churches Assembly 1991: www.cta-usa.org/foundationdocs/foundhyunkyung.html);
- tentative, open-ended conclusions.

We can take one example to illustrate some of these points. Joy Mead is a member of the Iona community and her poem on the story of Shiphrah and Puah (Exod. 1) explores how the midwives open up possibilities of acting differently from what was expected, collaborating rather than competing, 'trusting vulnerability' and disobeying orders (Mead 2002, pp. 43–4). Mead's reading of the story draws out the possibilities available to us when our power seems to be restricted. It encourages us to question dominant thinking and to see disobedience as a valid ethical choice. Mead explores how these two women worked together to ensure the survival of the babies and asks how we might also be midwifes to hope through small everyday actions.

Try it out

Read through a text you are working on and note down any ways in which you think your interpretation is affected by your gender and sexuality. What is hidden? What aspects of the text are brought into focus? What conversation about this text would you want to have with someone of the opposite gender or a different sexual orientation?

Ethnicity

> ### Try it out
>
> At the start of this section you are encouraged to spend time thinking about your ethnicity before reading on. You might also want to explore your nationality and family background. How do you feel about this aspect of your identity? How do you think it might affect your reading of the Bible?

The importance of ethnicity is demonstrated in a comment by Ghanaian theologian Mercy Amba Oduyoye, 'I am first and foremost an Akan, a member of a matrilineal society speaking the language of Akan ... In fact it is as an African that I am a Christian' (Oduyoye 1990, p. 245). For Oduyoye, her ethnic identity is primary, even mediating her relationship with God. However, many white Christians are not used to thinking about their ethnic identity and might struggle to describe how it influences their reading of the Bible. If white people do have any ethnic awareness, it tends to be accompanied by guilt about their own or others' racism or denial that it makes a difference to their interpretation. The predominantly white ethnicity of biblical scholars from the dominant tradition has been hidden but has nevertheless had a huge impact on the way the Bible has been interpreted and taught. Randall Bailey admits to fellow African-Americans:

> we read the text with the interests of whites, who are our oppressors, in mind. We, who have had our land stolen and have been enslaved by the people who stole our land, read the promise to Abraham to be given someone else's land and don't see our own story. We identify with Abraham. (Bailey 1998, p. 78)

How then does our ethnic identity shape our reading of the Bible? Again, we note a few suggestions of how this aspect of our identity might influence our interpretation.

To begin with, an awareness of ethnic identity (particularly for white people who have been socialized into assuming they do not have a skin colour) should help readers acknowledge the ethnic reality of the biblical context. The ethnic identity of biblical characters and communities can go unnoticed unless the text reports a conflict situation between different ethnic groups. But the Bible is not a blank canvas. Its context is North Africa, Asia, the Middle East and, in later New Testament texts, some southern Mediterranean countries. For white European readers recalling this geographical reality should guard against the domestication and Europeanization of the Bible.

Descriptions of ethnic conflict with the narrative will be experienced differently by readers who are living in areas of ethnic tension. They may be more alert to the violence and disruption that accompanies such disputes. Readers living in politically stable contexts might reflect on the role played by outsiders in ethnic conflict: What is the catalyst for division? How is conflict triggered by poverty and exclusion? Within the Bible, the relationship between ethnic groups is ever-changing. The identity of the dominant and oppressed fluctuates throughout biblical history. At times the Israelites are oppressed by other nations or ethnic groups such as the Egyptians, Babylonians or Romans. But at other times it is they who attack and subjugate other ethnic groups such as the Canaanites or Samaritans. Some communities have found it necessary to read the Bible from a counterposition: for example, Puerto Rican and First Nations theologians reading from a history of invasion have identified with groups such as the Ammonites rather than the Israelites when hearing the stories of the conquest of Canaan. This narrative of conflict and oppression continues into readers' own lives and this should encourage them to explore whether the Bible offers appropriate models of reconciliation.

Anti-Semitism has been a shameful feature of Christian biblical study since early on in the history of the church. Christian readers of the Bible will need to be alert to the impact history (see Chapter 5) of texts about the Jews within John's Gospel, for example. The village of Oberammergau in South Germany is an example of a community that has begun to critique its anti-Semitic legacy of interpretation. Earlier versions of the Passion Play (held every ten years in Oberammergau) were marked by anti-Jewish interpretations: Hitler demonstrated his support for the play when he attended a performance in 1934. However, for the performance in the year 2000, the village decided to challenge its reading of the Gospel. The millennium version was defined by a shift that differentiated between the Jewish people and the religious leaders. Furthermore, the responsibility of Judas for the death of Christ was placed on all peoples through the suggestion that Judas was abandoned to his actions by the other disciples who did not seek him out when he went astray. For more details see: www.passionsspiele2000. de/passnet/english/index_e.html

Christian and Jewish readers both need to engage responsibly with the doctrine of election, which has been used to justify the suppression of a range of religious and ethnic groups. Readers of dominant ethnic communities and nations need to be alert to the dangers of an uncritical doctrine of chosenness. Yet even within the canon, there is a clear tradition that relates the Israelites' election to a responsibility to serve the wider world. This strand endorses a theology of God's universal love. The story of Jonah is a good example of such a debate within the Bible, since scholars believe it was written as a response to the nationalistic tendencies of the books of Nehemiah and Ezra. Jonah, as a representative of the Israelites, learns to value the despised pagan city of Nineveh. Indeed, it is Nineveh that demonstrates true repentance and faith in God.

Black communities suffering under white supremacy have challenged traditional interpretations that have validated racist oppression, for example, readings of the curse of Ham in Genesis 9.20–27 that identify Ham as black. These communities have also recovered positive identifications of black ethnic identify. They have argued for Song of Songs 1.5 to be accurately translated as 'I am black and beautiful' rather than former interpretations of the verse as 'I am black but beautiful'. There is a counter-tradition of interpretation that upholds the Bible as a source of liberation for groups suffering racism. Randall Bailey notes the longstanding identification of African-Americans with the Exodus narrative. He cites as an example the spiritual, *Go Down Moses* sung by slaves in ante-bellum America:

When Israel was in Egypt land,
Let my people go.
Oppressed so hard they could not stand,
Let my people go.

Go down, Moses, way down to Egypt land.
Tell ole Pharaoh to let my people go.
(Cited in Bailey 1998, p. 67)

To demonstrate further how ethnic identity shapes biblical interpretation, we turn to an example from Kevin Smith's film *Dogma* (1999). In it, Rufus, a man claiming to be the thirteenth apostle, explains the politics of ethnicity in the Bible. Rufus is black and suggest this is the reason he was written out of the gospel narrative. He goes on to argue that Jesus was also black but the early church felt this would be detrimental to the spread of the gospel so ordered all images of Jesus to portray him as a European with blonde hair and blue eyes.

Smith, a white filmmaker, uses *Dogma* to reinterpret his Catholic upbringing. He critiques the 'whitewashing' of Jesus over the centuries. Richard Dyer in his book *White* notes a shift in flesh colourization in paintings of Jesus from the medieval to the Renaissance period, from a general 'pinky-yellowy' to registering different skin colours (Dyer 1997, p. 66). From the Renaissance, Christ was increasingly rendered as paler than other figures who took on darker appearances, becoming darker the further they were from Christ, both physically and symbolically. This period of art reflected European expansion and conquest of other lands, notably in the crusades against Arab Muslims. The crusades added to European associations of white with Christianity and salvation; and black with other religions and peoples, with sin and death. Over the centuries the whitening of Christ increased, reaching a climax by the nineteenth century of a fair-skinned, blonde-haired blue-eyed Christ (see also Stephen Moore's *God's Beauty Parlor and Other Queer Spaces in and Around the Bible* (2001)). Enlightenment theories placed white-skinned people at the pinnacle of human development, suggesting they were the most beautiful, most intellectual, and most virtuous of all people. Thus Christ's perfection was taken to mean that he too must be whiter than white. Contemporary readers of the Bible often need to work hard to overcome such racist identifications in their interpretations.

Try it out

Read through a text you are working on and note down any ways in which you think your interpretation is affected by your ethnicity. What is hidden? What aspects of the text are brought into focus? What conversation about this text would you want to have with someone of a different ethnic origin?

If the text you are working with is from one of the Gospels, look at a picture of a Christ of a different ethnic origin from you to help you explore these issues. How is your imagining of the passage transformed? A useful resource for this is *The Christ We Share* pack produced by CMS, USPG and the Methodist Church that contains images of Christ from around the world. Online, the Asian Christian Art organization provides a gallery of biblical images from this region: www.asianchristianart.org (click on 'Galleries' tab).

Age, ability and well-being

Try it out

Begin this section by noting your age, mental and physical abilities and state of health. How do you feel about this aspect of your identity? How do you think it might affect your reading of the Bible?

In comparison with gender and ethnicity, there has been much less work on how age and physical ability may affect a reader's interpretation of Scripture. Perhaps this is because of the fluid nature of these characteristics, since we change physically and mentally as we journey through life. This fluctuating element to our identity offers us a number of different perspectives on a passage. We will understand a story differently as a child, a young person, a parent or a retired person. Furthermore our physical and mental state will leave us open to different responses to the text.

> **Try it out**
>
> Read one short biblical passage every day for a week. How does your own changing physical and mental state affect your reading of the text?

We have different needs and desires as we move through different states of age, ability and health. Consider for example, how mourners at a funeral respond to biblical texts such as John 14.1–7 at a time when they seek comfort and hope. There are other ways in which these temporary characteristics impact biblical interpretation, to which we now turn.

At different stages of their lives readers identify more readily with different characters. The Bible offers stories about a range of characters and life situations: Samuel – a boy waiting for guidance in the temple; Sarah – an old woman surprised by her ability to have a child; a nameless widow offering what little she had; a blind man healed by his encounter with Jesus. While culturally specific, there are few human rites of passage or life situations not reflected within the canon.

However, for contemporary readers, the biblical assessment of different life events may differ from their understanding of similar situations. They may no longer accept the age-related cultural associations of the Bible. Children may not be understood as a reward or childlessness as a curse. Few people in western secular society regard disability as the result of sin. Greater scientific and medical knowledge has altered attitudes to the healing miracles. Readers, therefore, need to negotiate the cultural attitudes of the narrative in order to let it speak to today's context.

Awareness of their physical and mental state should help readers question methods of exclusion practised within the biblical context and employed today. The HIV/AIDS pandemic has created new readings of biblical texts. While some churches have excluded people with AIDS, rejecting them as sinners, others have taken Jesus' special concern for lepers as their model of engagement. (There is an example of such a reading in the section on globalization, p. 115 below.) As another example, the purity laws of Leviticus should alert readers to the dangers of demanding physical perfection and enable them to challenge western society's 'body fascism' and fascination with the beautiful. In contrast, readers should note the countertradition within the Bible that chooses the second-born, weakest, or cultically 'imperfect' person over the obvious heroes, e.g. the young David is the surprise choice in the search for the new king (1 Sam. 16). What does this tradition suggest to readers of the text?

Readers from different cultural contexts may also have different responses to the healing stories in the Bible. In reading the story of the man with the withered hand (Mark 3.1–6), Tiffany and Ringe suggest that educated western readers apply their medical and scientific worldview to the story and are sceptical about the miraculous nature of the event. Their reading becomes a search for a rational explanation. However, readers from contexts where traditional medicine is practised are usually more accepting of the story and make connections between methods of healing practised in their own community. Finally, people with disabilities might challenge the assumptions of the narrator that the goal for each individual is to be able-bodied (Tiffany and Ringe 1996, pp. 182–3).

People who are differently abled have provided new insights into these and other passages. Some have argued for the need to take pride in their physical state and the unique insights it offers. For example, John Hull reflects on the insights his blindness has given him as a reader of the Bible in his book, *In the Beginning There Was Darkness: A blind person's conversations with the Bible* (2001). Jennie Weiss Block lists some of the ways in which people with disabilities have reinterpreted Scripture. She notes, 'Sometimes people with disabilities feel as though they are objectified in the disability Scripture passages, as if the only purpose they serve is to be healed' (Block 2002, p. 105). Block and others challenge the healing tradition within the church that can lead to judgements on a sick person's faith if they are not healed. She argues the main focus of Jesus' ministry was the restoration of wholeness to people rather than making people physically better. Block also notes how Jesus' wounds are not removed in his resurrected state: 'He showed his scars openly and without shame for they were, and remain, a sign of his humanity and the fullness of his life experience' (Block 2002, p. 109). As a further example, Elizabeth Lain Schell in her imaginative reading of Luke 13.10–17 suggests that the bent-over woman of the story became so through her attentive care towards her local community and, once healed, mourned the loss of her closeness to the ground. In this reading, the woman says about her healing:

> I'm glad to be straight again. Glad to look beyond my home, glad to look beyond the hills ... to feel the sunshine on my face. But I'm glad to feel my feet upon the ground. Glad to remember to look down now and then and see the things around me ... I've been here, stooped or straight, looking to God in my different ways. (Schell 1998, p. 52)

Try it out

Read through a text you are working on and note down any ways in which you think your interpretation is effected by your physical and mental state. What is hidden? What aspects of the text are brought into focus? What conversation about this text would you want to have with someone of a different age, ability or state of health?

Socio-economic status and political affiliation

Try it out

Describe your social status and economic situation. What is your political affiliation? How do you think these features of your identity affect your reading of the Bible?

We have already explored how when poor communities read the Bible they rejoice in its message of good news. Furthermore, we have observed how liberation theologians argue that reading from the margins enables us to see things hidden from those nearer the centres of power. We have also considered how politics and ideology have shaped the use of the Bible over the centuries. We turn now to a few further examples of how these realities might impact our reading.

Inevitably, readers from different socio-economic contexts have different blind spots to the stories of the Bible, e.g. only some readers will be able to understand the despair of the debtor in Jesus' parable. There has been much work done on recovering the socio-economic reality of the Bible to help prevent misreadings of the text. We look at these interpretative methods in Chapter 5.

Politicians from across the spectrum value the Bible and even refer to it in support of their (opposing) policies. As one example, the Conservative Christian Fellowship is a group of Christians involved in the Conservative Party in the United Kingdom. Their website demonstrates how the Bible impacts on their agenda:

> Everyday experience confirms the value of the Bible's moral wisdom: the best route out of poverty is to work, stay out of crime and honour marriage. In other words, personal responsibility is our first defence against social injustice. Experience also warns us that the existence of social injustice undermines personal integrity. Debt, unemployment and lack of shelter, for example, put enormous pressure on community and family solidarity. www.ccfwebsite.com/mission_page.php?ID=1

Try it out

Read Matthew 22.1–14, the parable of the wedding feast. How might readers' political persuasions influence their reading of this parable? (You could think about the different interpretations that may be offered by a monarchist, a republican, a member of the military or a pacifist). Why do you think some interpreters avoid using the term 'kingdom of God'?

Elsa Tamez notes, 'The poor find that the Word reaffirms in a clear and direct way that God is with them in their fight for life' (Tamez 1995, p. 50). If poor people read the Bible with a sense of affirmation, what is the experience of the rich? Readers who are financially secure might feel guilty or threatened as they read some passages. However, wealth accumulation and possession are regarded in a variety of ways in the Scriptures. While Amos might curse the profiteering market traders, the accumulation of vast riches by Solomon (through, among other methods, forced labour) appears as a sign of God's blessing.

To explore some of these themes further, consider how a financially secure person might read the story of Jesus' encounter with the rich young man (Mark 10.17–22). A wealthy reader might be deeply challenged by this story. Jesus' teaching on wealth is consistent throughout the Gospels: riches inhibit a person's discipleship. Rich readers might reflect on how their wealth affects their faith journey. How has their wealth enabled or prevented them to live rightly before God? Stanley Hauerwas' argument that discipleship is about dispossession would fit well with this narrative – the rich young man is asked to give up his financial security and take the risk of following Jesus.

Yet an American scholar, Sondra Ely Wheeler argues the New Testament is not anti-materialist. Rather:

> Material wealth is problematic because it is often a hindrance to heeding the gospel; it is dangerous because it is a temptation to the sin of idolatry; it is suspect because it is frequently the result or the means of social injustice; finally, its disposition is a matter of great moral weight, as the response to human needs is a sign of the advent of God's kingdom and the text of love that identifies Jesus' true followers. (Wheeler 1995, p. 134)

Wheeler suggests that if these concerns are adequately dealt with, there is no reason why the rich cannot be true followers of Christ. However, she points out the pivotal importance of sharing resources within the early church and warns affluent communities to take seriously this model of being church.

Try it out

Read through the text you are working on and note down any ways in which you think your interpretation is effected by your socio-economic status and political allegiance. What is hidden? What aspects of the text are brought into focus? What conversation about this text would you want to have with someone of a different socio-economic status or political allegiance?

Denominational, spiritual and theological traditions

Try it out

If you belong to a faith community, describe your denominational identity and the spiritual and theological traditions you feel part of. How do you think these features of your identity affect your reading of the Bible?

The attitude of Christians to the Bible is no longer divided along denominational lines, with each denomination encompassing a broad range of theological perspectives. However, the weight of denominational culture is still felt on members and continues to shape attitudes to the Bible and key texts within them. Reading with an awareness of denominational attitudes towards Scripture increases readers' awareness of the accepted interpretations of a text within a faith community.

Although all mainstream denominations regard the Bible as authoritative, they differ in the way they relate the Bible to other sources of knowledge. Roman Catholics place greater emphasis on the church's teaching (tradition) alongside Scripture. The reformed tradition tends towards the doctrine of *sola scriptura*. Methodist thinking has been compared to a mobile with the Bible at the centre and the three other elements of Wesley's Quadrilateral (experience, tradition and reason) suspended around the Bible. Thus the Bible remains central but there is an acknowledgement of the role of other sources of knowledge in reading the text. Readers need to take account of such understandings of the Scriptures as a source of revelation and recognize how they prevent or enable dialogue with the text.

Each denomination holds some texts closer to its heart than others. These are texts that have been formative in the shaping of the denomination's identity. The reformed tradition is profoundly influenced by Paul's letter to the Romans, and Luther's interpretation of the doctrine of 'justification by faith'. Roman Catholic identity is embedded in Jesus' confirmation of Peter as the rock on which the church is built (Matthew 16.17–19). Theological doctrines have a huge impact on readings of a text, although this is often not acknowledged. John Stackhouse warns of the lack of awareness about how theological doctrines shape biblical interpretation, noting how, for example, the 'dispensationsalist believes that such a system is merely the end result of careful exegesis, not a paradigm that, once adopted, bends recalcitrant texts to its pattern' (Stackhouse 2004, p. 188).

The desire to maintain orthodoxy has affected biblical studies throughout the history of the church. Brueggemann suggests that the Protestant reformers wrestled the biblical text from controlling church dogma and moved from what should be said about God in the Bible to what was said about God in the Bible (Brueggemann 1997b, p. 2). However this moment of emancipation was not sustained and a more open interpretative approach was compromised in turn by the reformers' own theological arguments. A prior commitment to defend doctrinal claims can prevent us from taking seriously texts that challenge these claims. Brueggemann warns, 'some of the most interesting and most poignant aspects of the Old Testament do not conform to or are not easily subsumed under church theology' (Brueggemann 1997b, p. 106).

Changes in church practice have also impacted biblical readings. For example, new readings of passages relating to the early church have arisen from changing patterns of ministry. The report to the Methodist Conference (2004) on the diaconate illustrates how developing understandings of this ministry have led to a revision of traditional interpretations of a biblical word. While a deacon's ministry was traditionally associated with humble service, new interpretations have demonstrated that deacons in the New Testament also had an ambassadorial role, acting as a bridge-builder and provoking change (The Methodist Church 2004, p. 4.5). In this example, ecclesiology influenced the way a passage is read, challenging long-accepted translations of a word in an attempt to free up new ways of ministering in the world.

Try it out

Read through a text you are working on and note down any ways in which you think your interpretation is affected by your denominational identity and theology and spirituality as appropriate. What is hidden? What aspects of the text are brought into focus? What conversation about this text would you want to have with someone of a different denomination, theology or spiritual tradition?

Reading our situation

This next section is concerned with how biblical interpretation is influenced by the lived situation of the audience or reader (where the reader is as well as who they are). This section will also briefly introduce social analysis and its value for biblical interpretation.

In Chapter 3 we noted how redaction criticism examines the ways that the editor or redactor of a book or section of the Bible has shaped the original material or account to make it speak to their context. For some parts of the Hebrew Bible, there may have been several redactors, each shaping the tradition. Thus, the process of retelling a story to make a theological or political comment began while the books of the Bible were still being created. This means that the tradition has always been interpreted and framed in the light of the needs of a contemporary community. Directing the tradition to engage with the present reality cannot be dismissed as a recent trend.

Social analysis

The recognition that biblical editors related the tradition to their context, prompts us to consider how we might also understand the context in which we read the Bible.

Social analysis is a vital skill for biblical interpreters, even if we do not consider ourselves to have the necessary training in sociology, anthropology, economics, etc. In order for us to speak coherently and meaningfully as biblical interpreters, we must try to understand the context for which we interpret. We might think, for example, of the kind of support a local church should offer a family in which the breadwinner has been made redundant through the closure of a local manufacturing plant. The church would need to have some understanding of social and economic issues such as global employment patterns, social security and state provision, retraining and vocation. The community should then be more able to bring the biblical narrative (teaching and stories about work and community) into dialogue with the social reality.

Joe Holland and Peter Henriot define social analysis as, 'the effort to obtain a more complete picture of a social situation by exploring its *historical and structural relationships*. Social analysis serves as a tool that permits us to grasp the reality with which we are dealing' (Holland and Henriot 1983, p. 15 their italics). They further note that such analysis can focus on particular issues, policies or underlying structures. It takes into consideration political order, economic systems and cultural foundations. Social analysts may also consider how the social context has changed over a period of time and what conclusions can be drawn about the possible shape of future social developments.

One of the fundamental differences between liberation theology and classical theology is that liberation theology takes action in the world as its starting point, rather than reflection or theory. Indeed, when it first appeared, Gustavo Gutiérrez's *A Theology of Liberation* was heavily criticized for being too concerned with social analysis rather than traditional theological themes. Liberation theologians continue to use their daily reality as a viable starting point for their reflections, e.g. the Ecumenical Association of Third World Theologians (EATWOT) begins its conferences by visiting and talking with local people about their reality.

Try it out

Look at one of the following resources to see how theologians use social analysis as a basis for theological reflection:

An EATWOT publication or its journal, *Voices from the Third World*
The Council for World Mission Theological Enquiry website: www.cwmnote.org
The World Council of Churches Assembly website: www.wcc-assembly.info

How then do we accurately read the signs of the times (a phrase popularized by Latin American theologians)? What skills do we need to acquire in order to do this? The see–judge–act method used by liberation theologians arose from Catholic social movements in the 1960s. It begins with being attentive to a situation (sometimes using social analysis tools such as interviews, and other methods of data collection). This observation is followed by evaluation of data and critical reflection on findings – often through a specific lens, e.g. economic or gender justice issues. Finally an active response is required in order to enable social change. While liberation theologians initially used Marxist theory for their analysis, contemporary social theologians are not wedded to any one method of social analysis.

If this all sounds too complicated, let's take a simple example of social (in this case environmental) observation, analysis and action. Tove Jansson's *The Summer Book* (first published 1973) records the relationship between an elderly woman and her six-year-old granddaughter as they spend the summer on a tiny island in the Gulf of Finland. In the following extract, we have an example of close analysis of the natural environment and human impact on it:

> Except for the magic forest, the island became an orderly, beautiful park. They tidied it down to the smallest twig while the earth was still soaked with spring rain, and, after that, they stuck carefully to the narrow paths that wandered through the carpet of moss from one granite outcropping to another and down to the sand beach. Only farmers and summer guests walk on the moss. What they don't know – and it cannot be repeated too often – is that moss is terribly frail. Step on it once and it rises the next time it rains. The second time, it doesn't rise back up. And the third time you step on moss, it dies. (Jansson 2003, pp. 28–9)

Careful observation and a commitment to the well-being of the island enabled the protagonists to make judgements about the actions of the farmers and guests and to modify their own behaviour accordingly.

Listening to a situation

All social analysis begins with careful observation. Within this field, one figure stands out as instrumental in developing a method of socially committed observation and evaluation. Paulo Freire (1921–97) was an influential Brazilian educationalist whose ideas (outlined in *Pedagogy of the Oppressed*, first published 1973) were tested out during literacy programmes among rural communities. Freire observed how the peasants he was working with had lost trust in their own ability to evaluate their reality:

> They call themselves ignorant and say the 'professor' is the one who has knowledge and to whom they should listen ... almost never do they realize that they, too, 'know things' they have learned in their relations with the world and with other women and men. (Freire 1993, p. 45)

He therefore developed a method of education that enabled participants to describe their reality and thus provide the basic resources for their own education. Freire's method of analysis and action can be summarized as such:

- Start from the concerns of the learners.
- Draw out individuals' experiences.
- Look for shared patterns of experience and knowledge.
- Explore the dynamics of power in the situation.
- Name the situation, ask questions and identify problems.
- Envisage a changed future and explore the consequences of that vision.
- Plan for collective action.
- Act!
- Reflect, evaluate and discover further questions.

The informal education site www.infed.org has more information on Freire's theory and other popular education methods.

Freire's method highlights the importance of beginning with lived experience. This means that our analysis of a situation must begin with those who live in it by asking them about their hopes and concerns. The next step is to identify emerging patterns between each individual's experience. The group is then helped to see wider social patterns and their impact (conscientization) which empowers them to work for social change.

Although there are many specialized tools and skills involved in academic social analysis, this does not prevent us from having a go for ourselves. We can begin with careful, thoughtful observation of a situation via our own experiences and through dialogue with others. Of course, other resources such as census returns, local records and social analyses completed by different organizations or academics are very valuable when available to complement our own observations. There are also a number of books on practical theology that include guidelines for social research.

The following checklist offers some initial areas for consideration when attempting to read a situation:

Social context

- Demography (population make up and distribution), including changing patterns (e.g. in gender balance; ethnic mix; age) and relationships.
- Characteristics of, and relationship between, urban, rural and suburban areas.
- Housing provision and the level of homelessness.
- Education provision, access and standard.
- Health and healthcare.
- Food production and eating patterns.
- Environmental pollution and destruction.

Economic context

- Economic health and the availability and distribution of resources: natural, financial and human.
- Wealth distribution, the difference between rich and poor, and the number of people living below the poverty line.
- Employment, under-employment and unemployment; average wage levels; the power relationship between workers and management.

Political context

- Political spectrum.
- Dominant ideology.
- Level of democracy and freedom of expression.
- Distribution of social power and influence.
- Politics of inclusion or exclusion; human rights.

Cultural context

- Media ownership and output.
- Cultural diversity and the amount of dialogue between different cultural groups.
- Art and expression.

- Sport and recreation.
- Fringe or subcultures; excluded groups; definition of anti-social or counter-cultural.

Methods of Analysis

There are a number of resources available to help us develop our social aware-ness and begin to 'read' a situation. Evaluative methods tend to be rooted in particular ideologies (e.g. Marxist analysis) that govern how they interpret social data and the social changes and goals they advocate. Theologians will also want to reflect on the situation, using theological themes and resources to evaluate the context. From a theological perspective, social analysis is 'a deliberate team effort to investigate and evaluate the conditions of life (eco-nomic, political, cultural, etc.) of one's own community, or the community one is committed to, in order to transform such conditions in accordance with God's liberating plan' (Maduro 2000, p. 185).

Holland and Henriot (1983, pp. 98–100) offer one method for theologians. In summary it requires the following steps:

- Mapping social development and change;
- Identifying critical incidents that have provoked change;
- Identifying the underlying structures of a situation: how society organizes resources; power; relationships and meaning;
- Analysing dominant and alternative value systems;
- Imagining future developments and social change.

They suggest theologians should evaluate a social context through asking:

- What reinforces gospel values, social teachings, etc.?
- What undercuts, destroys these values and these teachings?
- Where is Jesus present here?
- What are 'signs of the kingdom' in this situation?
- What is *grace* in this situation, as an opening up to God?
- What is *sin* in this situation, as a turning from God?
- What does 'salvation' mean in this situation? (Holland and Henriot 1983, pp. 104–5)

Globalization

Any discussion of our social context, however brief, must make mention of globalization – a determinative factor in our contemporary reality. Charities like Christian Aid and CAFOD define globalization in the following way:

> Globalisation is a process of increasing interconnectedness of individuals, groups, companies and countries. The technological, economic and political changes which have brought people closer together have also generated serious concerns over the terms of that integration. These concerns have been generated by the realisation that while globalisation has led to benefits for some, it has not led to benefits for all. The benefits appear to have gone to those who already have the most, while many of the poorest have failed to benefit fully and some have even been made poorer. (Green and Melamed 2000)

As evidence of this growing disparity, a 2004 Christian Aid report, drawing from UN statistics, noted that fifty-four countries were poorer than they were in 1990 (Christian Aid 2004, p. 16).

In a globalized world, we read the Bible from a global perspective – our location is the whole world. This does not mean it is possible to read the Bible in a way that suggests everyone has the same experience and desires as oneself. Living in the world as a 'global citizen' actually increases the need to be specific about social and economic location. We become acutely aware of the great differences between the world's inhabitants. We, therefore, have to understand how we stand in relation to others, while at the same time recognizing the common links and therefore our common interests.

Try it out

Identify one particular environmental concern (e.g. climate change, deforestation, access to clean water), then read Genesis 1 through that lens. What response do you have to the text when you focus on the reality of your environmental location?

Our example for this section on social context considers the impact of the AIDS pandemic on reading the Bible. In his article, 'Reading the Bible in the Light of HIV/AIDS in South Africa', Gerald West draws on the experience of popular Bible study groups attended by people who are HIV positive. West notes how even the group's choice of passage is affected by their situation:

> The group usually chose texts in which Jesus was speaking and/or acting over against the prevailing views of society. In other words, the texts chosen for Bible study tended to be those texts in which socially normative views victimized certain people, who were then affirmed and dignified and reinserted into a reconstituted society by Jesus. (West 2003, p. 338)

He observes how the group members seem to suffer more on account of emotional rejection than physical illness. They are judged by society – even when they die their funerals become arenas of judgement. However, the Gospels' portrayal of Jesus helps them challenge their social exclusion. As an example, through studying the story of Jesus' encounter with the woman allegedly caught in adultery (John 8.1–11) members of the group were affirmed and accepted: 'The Jesus of this text had entered into and reconstituted the counselling encounter, bringing forgiveness, healing and acceptance' (West 2003, p. 343).

Our social reality shapes our selection of passages to study, the questions we bring to the text and the interpretation we place on it. As we learn about our location in the world, we come to understand how we are placed within the structures of our social reality. Are we one of the powerful? How is our power restricted? With whom do we form our allegiances? Are we comfortable with our position in society or do we wish to challenge it?

Reading in community

All of us belong to groups that, even if not communities of faith, influence how we interpret the Bible. Our belonging offers us opportunities and responsibilities. We commit ourselves to particular groups within society; these are our communities of accountability. Our communities are those people we journey with. They are the people with whom we test out our interpretation of Scripture. It is these groups that we most often bring into our dialogue with the text.

> ## Try it out
>
> Identify your communities of accountability. Now consider some of these diagnostic questions:
> - Are these communities based on gender, ethnicity, denomination, profession, or class?
> - Does loyalty to one group create tension with another group?
> - How might you be a prophet within these communities?
> - How is your interpretation influenced by these communities?
> - What responsibilities do you feel towards these communities when interpreting the Bible?

Many anthropologists and theologians regard humans as fundamentally relational and social beings, existing only in relation to others. This relational aspect to human identity has an impact on the location and method of biblical interpretation. Sandra Schneiders comments:

Since the Bible is the product of a community experience and is meant to nourish and guide the community of believers, it is helpful to share biblical study and prayer with others. Because every great text has multiple meanings and layers of significance, different dimensions of meaning will be discovered by different readers. Furthermore, sharing interpretations minimizes the chances of totally erroneous or idiosyncratic reading. (Schneiders 1997)

> ## Try it out
>
> When and where do you read or discuss the Bible with other people? Your list might include: lectures; Bible study groups; family meal times; worship; down the pub. Reflect on the process of reading with others. What new insights are enabled? How does the group deal with conflicting interpretations of a passage?

The church as an interpretative community

For Christians and Jews, the believing community is the primary group in which the Bible is explored. As we saw in Chapter 2, the Bible as Christian canon was formed by the church and, in the first instance, for the church. In response, the church is formed and transformed around the Bible. Because of this special relationship, the church has a responsibility to interpret the Bible. Interpretation of the texts is part of its calling and identity.

The church interprets the Bible in its preaching, teaching, worship and action, proclaiming it in fresh and relevant ways (World Council of Churches 1998, p. 19). One of the most important ways the church lives out the Bible is in the celebration of Holy Communion (also called the Mass, Eucharist or the Lord's Supper). This central act of worship recalls the last supper of Jesus with his disciples and is a time of fellowship, renewal and recommitment. The service traditionally follows the pattern of the biblical accounts with believers participating in the sharing of the bread and wine, as the first disciples did:

> Holy God, we praise you
> that on the night in which he was betrayed
> our Saviour Christ took bread
> and gave you thanks.
> He broke it, and gave it to his disciples, saying,
> 'Take, eat. This is my body, given for you.
> Do this in remembrance of me.'
>
> After supper, he took the cup of wine,
> gave thanks, and gave it to them, saying,
> 'Drink from it, all of you.
> This is my blood of the new covenant,
> poured out for all people
> for the forgiveness of sins.
> Do this in remembrance of me.'
> (The Methodist Church 1999, p. 193)

Some Christian scholars believe the church is the only correct context for biblical interpretation. A well-known advocate of this view is the North American Methodist scholar Stanley Hauerwas. Hauerwas is insistent that the Bible should only be read from the midst of a believing community, arguing that 'the Bible without the community, without expounders, and interpreters, and hearers is a dead book' (Hauerwas 1983, p. 98). Indeed Hauerwas argues it is only within a community that is shaped by the Bible that the Bible can be made known. Thus the church's primary role is to perform or live out the biblical narrative.

We might argue that such a community-focused method of interpretation leaves churches open to collective ignorance as much as collective wisdom. In response Hauerwas suggests that the Bible:

> stands over the community exerting a critical function, but that it does so is an aspect of the community's self-understanding. Scripture is the means the church uses to constantly test its memory. That is why it can never be content with using just one part of Scripture, but must struggle day in and day out with the full text. For the story the church must tell as well as embody is a many-sided tale which constantly calls us from complacency and conventions. (Hauerwas 1983, p. 98)

Hauerwas believes the canon itself has the resources to challenge its interpreters. In Chapter 6 we will consider further this question of whether the Bible can be read against ourselves. For now, it is worth noting how difficult it is to do this.

Richard Bauckham points out the need for individual members of a community to have freedom to offer new and challenging readings, to 'allow for the Jeremiahs and the Luthers' (Bauckham 1999, p. 22). Again, we should note the difficulty of ensuring this safeguard. It is hard for individuals to go against the group mentality and perhaps harder for the community to hear and respond to criticism.

The church's diverse nature inevitably creates diverse readings. Randy Litchfield advocates a middle way between extreme individualism in which no one has anything to say to each other; and enforced uniformity which suppresses real complexity of different identities (Litchfield 2004, p. 232). The Bible should act as a 'centering force' in Christian communities (Litchfield 2004, p. 226), holding diverse people together and recognized by all as a text to attend to: 'This Bible-mediated conversation weaves individuals together into a tradition and community' (Litchfield 2004, p. 228).

In recognition of the diverse contexts and local communities that make up the worldwide church, the World Council of Churches notes the importance of both contextuality, that is interpretation in response to the local situation; and catholicity, that is shared binding beliefs (World Council of Churches 1998, p. 31).

Try it out

The sixth commandment, 'You shall not kill' (Exod. 20.13) is agreed teaching for all Christians. Yet there is much division over the application of this notion of the sanctity of life. Think how the commandment is interpreted by Christians who advocate the death penalty, vegetarianism, pacifism, or the pro-life movement. Can even such a central teaching as this one function as a 'centring force'?

The benefits of reading together

Despite the difficulties, there are great gains to be had from studying the text together. The important thing is to commit to listening and learning from another's interpretation:

> The reading from another's location creates an awareness in me of the particularity, brokenness and implications of my own reading – and very likely also the associated discovery of commonalities. Issues of the truth of the text are thus located in a particular reading community but are also connected to other communities. (Litchfield 2004, p. 235)

As biblical interpreters, it is vital that we seek out other perspectives on a text. We need to remain open to the diversity of interpretations and this requires us to accept the reality of another person's location as well as the impact this has on their interpretation. The *Global Bible Commentary* argues that, 'It is only when we recognize the differences between our interpretation and those of others that we learn from them, and thus truly respect them – rather than co-opting them by pretending they are the same as ours, or rejecting them as meaningless. (Patte 2004, p. xxxvi).

David Rhoads (2005, p. 226) warns us never to trust ourselves to interpret the Bible correctly on our own. While recognizing the complexity of negotiating differences and redressing power imbalances between interpreters, Rhoads argues that reading interculturally is most likely to result in valid and relevant interpretations. In this section we have considered the differences within our own communities. By naming our community, diverse as it may be, we also acknowledge those groups to whom we do not belong. In the next chapter, we consider how best to hear the insights of those with alternative experiences and commitments to ours.

5

Committed Readings

Introduction: the influence of our commitments

In this chapter, we consider how our commitments affect the way we interpret the Bible. Our commitments arise out of our experience of our reality, our own needs and the needs of others. In recent years, many new critical tools have been developed to allow interpreters to read the Bible in a way that meets these needs. This is a welcome change since people have become impatient with ways of reading the Bible that yield nothing that is relevant to them, or people they care about.

Try it out

1 Think of a current situation in your life, which you would like to reflect on more deeply using the Bible as a dialogue partner. Write it down. Note how doing this brings your own life to the forefront of your mind.

2 Review the notes on your identity you developed in Chapter 4.

3 Find a passage that seems to relate to your situation and identity.

4 Read it, keeping your situation at the forefront of your mind and setting aside historical-critical questions. Write down any thoughts, observations or insights that come to you.

5 Now review your reading experience. In what ways, if any, does this passage give you insight into your situation?

6 Does this reading process reveal important gaps between you and the passage, e.g. that something important about your situation

is absent from the passage, or the passage proposes beliefs and convictions you do not share?

It sometimes seems as if both diachronic and synchronic approaches to the Bible never get round to addressing the real life questions that matter to people. This is a consequence of the long-standing tradition of approaching the Bible historically. For example, in the second volume of John Barton's *The Biblical World* (2002, p. 437), William Telford lists sixty-eight methods and approaches to biblical interpretation, classified into three categories: historical, literary and theological. These categories are in the normal order taken by historical criticism which begins with literary and historical questions about the Bible before tackling questions about the beliefs and commitments of the original writer(s) and reader(s). Historical-critical approaches usually stop there, leaving modern readers to make up their own minds about how these ancient beliefs and commitments relate to theirs.

However, this situation is now changing, and in this chapter we look at approaches which bring contemporary interests and commitments into conversation with the Bible. One label for this cluster of critical approaches which take contemporary commitments seriously is 'existential readings', a term used by Gorman (2001, p. 202). His map of these approaches further classifies them into two categories: those which trust the text, and those which are suspicious of it. But this distinction is unhelpful in so far as it conceals the fact that all interpreters approach the Bible with a mixture of suspicion and trust. It is, therefore, more useful to speak of committed approaches. All written texts, including the Bible, must be scrutinized because they are products of their time and place and hence need to be read with historical awareness. Equally, classic texts, including the Bible, may be trusted to continue to illuminate and inspire us, whatever our personal commitments.

A consequence of becoming more attuned to the commitments of others is that we begin to notice that all interpretations, even those that claim to offer an impartial view, are affected by certain commitments. This is particularly important to remember when reading commentaries, the format of which can encourage us to forget they are the work of a person with ideological beliefs and commitments. Commentaries are important, because they are the genre that biblical scholars most often use to share the results of their study of the Bible with others. Happily, as we noted in Chapter 4, western interpreters have increasingly recognized the degree to which their location and interests do affect their interpretations. Frequently they have learned this through listening to interpreters experiencing suffering, oppression or discrimination.

For example, as the struggle for majority government gained impetus in South Africa in the 1980s, there was a corresponding struggle between scholars focused on ever more intricate synchronic analyses of the Bible and those who insisted that it should contribute to the liberation struggle. With hindsight, it appears that those who were trying to limit the study of the Bible to literary questions about its structure and form were trying to distance themselves from the life experience of others who were striving for social and political liberation.

Approaches that address real contemporary interests and commitments fall into three broad categories:

- perspectives developed by biblical interpreters living in other cultures and contexts than the West;
- ideological perspectives developed to bring the core concerns of other disciplines into dialogue with the Bible;
- and faith perspectives concerned to interpret the Bible in ways that meet the needs of individuals seeking spiritual and moral guidance, or groups wishing to use such guidance to inform their collective public action.

They do not all assume or endorse one another, yet we shall see that they have much in common and there is considerable interaction between them.

World Perspectives

A generation ago the term 'world music' did not exist because the phenomenon to which it refers – a lively appreciation in the West for music from other parts of the world – did not exist. Now it is considered an important musical genre, with artists such as Ladysmith Black Mambazo gaining an enthusiastic following in many western countries. A similar shift has taken place in the realm of biblical studies. More and more western biblical scholars are actively listening to interpretations arising in other countries.

This attention to the insights of non-western readers marks a shift in emphasis, rather than an interpretative method, though a number of critical perspectives have risen to prominence through this change. Here we look at three types of interpretation: interpretation from parts of the world other than the West, postcolonial interpretations and vernacular interpretations.

Global collections

A growing number of major reference works now reflect a shift towards a global perspective on the Bible, as a brief survey of recent publications in this field demonstrates.

One of the first one-volume commentaries to draw contributions from all over the world was the *International Bible Commentary: A Catholic and Ecumenical Commentary for the Twenty-first Century* (1998) edited by William R. Farmer. Although the approach of most of the contributors still shows the strong influence of the historical-critical approach, the inclusion of voices and perspectives from all over the world widens its scope to include concerns such as healing, the family, workers' rights, violence, anti-Semitism and ecology. These pastoral concerns are also considered in supplementary articles within the commentary.

A second example of this trend is the *Global Bible Commentary* (2004) edited by a team of five scholars and offering readings on sections of each book of the Bible chosen on the basis of their relevancy to the life contexts of the interpreters drawn from all over the world. The introduction by the general editor Daniel Patte covers many of the issues dealt with in this Studyguide. Each entry begins with the life context of the interpretation before offering a contextual commentary and demonstrates how reading the text with the concerns of the context in mind has a profound impact on what is seen. For example, John Riches' reading of Ephesians is affected by reading this epistle in Scotland with the concerns of Scottish readers in mind. The prevalence of domestic violence in that context leads him and his co-readers to resist interpreting Ephesians 5.21–23 in a way that endorses views of headship or subordination in marriage (Riches in Patte 2004, p. 479).

A similar worldwide perspective is evident in the most recent *Dictionary of Biblical Interpretation*, edited by John H. Hayes (1999), which contains articles on biblical interpretation from all regions of the world. This global approach marks a real shift from another major dictionary on the same subject published just a decade earlier, *A Dictionary of Biblical Interpretation*, edited by R. J. Coggins and J. L. Houlden in 1990. Hayes not only includes African voices (absent from Coggins and Houlden's dictionary) but recognizes that it is no more possible to cover African biblical interpretation in one article than it would be to do so for Europe. There are many articles covering different aspects of biblical interpretation from around the world. Thus, as well as general articles considering how the Bible is interpreted in different geographical regions, there are also articles reviewing interpretative approaches arising out of:

- particular cultures, reflecting the complexity of readers' identity (e.g. Afrikaner interpretation, African-American interpretation, Afri-Carribean interpretation or Calypso interpretation);
- religious commitments (e.g. multifaith interpretation, Muslim interpretation, Jewish interpretation or Rastafarian interpretation);
- experiences of oppression (e.g. Dalit interpretation, Burakimin interpretation, Minjung interpretation, or South African black theology); or
- ideological concerns (e.g. androcentric interpretation, black interpretation, decolonial interpretation, or globalization and interpretation).

John Levison and Priscilla Pope-Levison's *Return to Babel: Global Perspectives on the Bible* (1999) offers a Latin American, African and Asian perspective on ten well-known biblical passages (Exod. 20, Ps. 23, Matt. 5, John 1, etc.). Each contributor looks first at his or her own context, then the text before producing a reflection on the passage. The process of starting with context acts as a filter for what is looked for exegetically within the text, and this in turn shapes the final hermeneutical reflections.

Helen Graham's Asian perspective on Matthew 5.1–12 offers an example of this process (Graham 1999, pp. 129–35). The context she describes in the Philippines is one of 'peacelessness' in the ongoing struggle between government forces and two revolutionary forces. This has led to the work of peace advocates in the countryside. This context brings into sharp focus Matthew 5.9 'Blessed are the peacemakers', and her exegetical investigation then discovers two hermeneutical keys. After the destruction of the second temple in 70 CE, a rabbi taught that 'the salvation formerly obtained through the peace offering could now be obtained through the peacemaker'. The beatitudes, and peacemaking in particular, offered Matthew's community a strategy of survival in a context in which they had been expelled from the Jewish assembly, but still wished to follow their alternative vision of Jewish society.

Using these insights, Graham's reflection shows how peace advocates were able to use Matthew 5.9, 'as a warrant for establishing a peace zone in an attempt to end the violence and free their energies for more creative endeavours'. She warns that such identification with the way of Jesus can be costly. In violent contexts peacemakers can lose their lives as 'peace offerings' (Graham 1999, p. 134).

Walter Dietrich and Ulrich Luz are the editors of a short collection called *The Bible in a World Context: An experiment in cultural hermeneutics* (2002), which explores cultural hermeneutics through Latin American, African and Asian readings of Luke 2. Elsa Tamez's contribution is sobering. She reminds readers that for many people in the world, the context in which they are living is becoming more life-threatening and hostile. At the start of the twenty-first century, unlike earlier decades, Latin American Christians now have to interpret the Bible in a context in which even belief in the possibility of social change has become absent.

Biblical scholarship alone does not have the resources to address this profound experience of powerlessness and loss of hope. Speaking poetically, she describes her context as living under a sky without stars and says that the stars, which represent hope, have to be sought everywhere: 'Search for them in the house, in the street, in institutions and organizations, within oneself and in the other' (Tamez 2002, p. 6).

Other studies aim to show how world biblical interpretation can affect popular understanding of the Bible. In the former category, is the collection on Revelation edited by David Rhoads, *From Every People and Nation: The book of Revelation in intercultural perspective* (2005). His use of the term 'intercultural' is similar to that of world biblical interpretation, but is more appropriate when the different cultural perspectives on a biblical book are all or mostly drawn from one country. Another feature of Rhoads' collection of intercultural studies of Revelation is its appendices, which explain the principles of intercultural Bible study and offer suggestions for group interaction, a checklist for readers to identify their own reading profile (similar to the process described in Chapter 4) and a group study guide to the book.

World biblical interpretation offers important insights to western readers. It alerts readers to the way globalization can make individuals also withdraw into individualism and become desensitized to stresses on their neighbours and environment. In the process, it does not neglect older historical-critical tools or newer approaches. World biblical interpretation makes regular use of sociological and rhetorical criticism to identify correspondences between the social and rhetorical situation addressed by the originators of the text, and contemporary recipients.

Postcolonial criticism

Postcolonial criticism interprets the Bible through the lens of colonialism. It focuses on 'expansion, domination and imperialism as central forces defining both the biblical narrative and biblical interpretation' and covers the overlapping areas of 'race, nation, translation, mission, textuality, spirituality and representation' as well as 'plurality, hybridity and postnationalism, the hallmarks of the postcolonial experience' (Sugirtharajah, 2002, p. 25). It is both a perspective which reads biblical texts through the experience of the colonized, and a critical method that uses postcolonial theory, poststructuralism and semiotics to critique other approaches to interpretation and the biblical texts themselves. By facing up to the ways in which domination, western expansion, and its ideological manifestations have defined the practices of biblical scholarship, it seeks to reshape the way the Bible is studied. R. S. Sugirtharajah is the leading advocate for this approach in the UK. He argues that it is way of moving beyond the limits of the approach of earlier liberation theology, which has lost its liberatory edge:

> In its appropriation of the Bible, in its expositions, in its obsession with Christ-centred hermeneutics, it [has] remained within conventional pat-

terns ... Instead of being a new agent in the ongoing work of God, liberation hermeneutics has ended up reflecting upon the theme of biblical liberation rather than being a liberative hermeneutics. (Sugirtharajah 2001, pp. 242–3)

For example, Kwok Pui-Lan contrasts the insights of white feminist interpreters with those of postcolonial critics into the story of the Syrophoenician woman in Mark 7.24–30 and Matthew 15.21–28:

> White feminist critics have moved her from the margin to the center by either reclaiming her as a foremother of gentile Christians or by praising her faith and her wit, which enables her to win the argument over Jesus and broaden Jesus' perspective towards the Gentiles. Postcolonial critics, however, emphasize that she is a women of other faith and her story is inscribed within the master discourse of the Christian canon and interpreted to justify mission to the Gentiles. (Kwok 2005, p. 65)

Similarly, when examining the history of interpretation of the characters of Rahab and Ruth, Kwok and other postcolonial interpreters such as Musa Dube note how Rahab and Ruth are only accepted as foreign, sexually active and resourceful women through their assimilation into the Israelite community (Kwok 2005, p. 82). When this imperialist perspective within the text is not critiqued by interpreters it can be problematic for the many Asian, African and Latin American women who have had little choice but to assimilate into a dominant culture through marriage or other means.

Postcolonial criticism also exposes the way anti-Semitic biblical interpretation has been used to encourage conversion in colonized nations. For example, during the evangelization of indigenous women, Jesus' egalitarian relationship with women may be presented as new and superior to patriarchal Jewish culture. Many postcolonial critics are more open to working across religious divisions, particularly valuing indigenous religions.

Postcolonial biblical criticism uses western exegetical tools, historical-critical and literary, against the very cultural traditions in which they were developed. Kwok notes that 'oppressed women have turned the Bible, a product introduced by the colonial officials, missionaries, and educators, into a site of contestation and resistance for their own emancipation' (Kwok

2005, pp. 77–8). Thus the approach calls into question both western cultural supremacy and the cultural supremacy of the Bible itself. Sugirtharajah writes:

> The purpose is not to recover in the biblical texts an alternative, or to search in its pages for a fresher way of coming to terms with the aftermath of colonial atrocity and trauma, and the current effects of globalization. The purpose is to interrupt the illusion of the Bible being the provider of all the answers, and to propose new angles, alternative directions, and interjections which will always have the victims and their plight as the foremost concern. (2002, pp. 101–2)

In saying this, Sugirtharajah reveals his awareness that traditional historical-critical methods still dominate in many parts of the world, even when interpreters try to draw on the resources offered by world, liberation, feminist or postcolonial interpreters. For example, David Joy's student handbook prepared in an Indian context, entitled *Revelation: A post-colonial viewpoint* (2001) is strikingly traditional. While he provides contextual illustrations and makes general statements about postcolonial conditions, these do not have much effect on his historical-critical reading of Revelation.

Try it out

Look up one of the passages describing the experience of non-Israelite women referred to above: Rahab from Canaan (Josh. 2), Ruth from Moab (Ruth 4.7–12) and the unnamed woman from Tyre (Mark 7.24–30 and Matt. 15.21–28).

- Ask yourself how these passages treat topics such as invasion, colonization and conquest. How do these texts view 'foreigners'? What is their view of the religious and cultural heritage of outsiders?
- Consult a standard historical-critical commentary to note the degree to which such commentaries deal with these politically important topics.
- Step back from the Bible and the commentaries and consider the ethical consequences of focusing or neglecting questions raised by postcolonial criticism.

Reading through the lens of local culture

Another branch of world biblical interpretation, vernacular hermeneutics, offers examples of how to interpret the Bible through the lens of local culture and is perhaps more accessible than postcolonial approaches to the Bible. It encourages interpreters to rediscover their own literary, cultural and religious heritage as a resource for understanding biblical ideas and narratives. As a method of biblical exegesis, it proceeds in three ways (Sugirtharajah 1999, pp. 97–103):

- by seeking textual or conceptual correspondences between biblical texts and local cultural traditions;
- by placing popular folk traditions (narratives, songs or sayings) alongside biblical materials in order to draw out the hermeneutical implications;
- and by using ritual and behavioural practices which are well known in the culture to illuminate the biblical text.

In such ways, it extends to all cultures the possibility of making their own valuable links with the biblical narrative. By favouring the indigenous and the local, by encouraging self-affirmation and self-esteem, and by opposing centralizing systems and theories, it gives strength and visibility to those most in danger of being swept away by the controlling, but often subtle, effects of western cultural imperialism. In these respects, it also bears a strong family resemblance to the perspective and procedures of impact history.

Vernacular Bible interpretation is often practised through seeing how ordinary people express their understanding of a biblical passage through art. For example, in South Africa Gerald West uses Azaria Mbatha's woodcut depicting the Joseph story to facilitate contextual Bible study of Genesis 37–50 (West in Sugirtharajah 1999, pp. 43–8). Mbatha's art is an example of the complexity of identifying what is local in our postmodern and globalized world. South African born and educated Mbatha has lived in Sweden for almost forty years, yet he is still feels himself to be close to the little village of Mabeka in Mahlabathini district of Kwazulu-Natal where he was born. He reminds us that 'Identity is not a question of geography' (Caroline Smart, http://www.artsmart.co.za/visual/archive/225.html 31 August 2005).

> **Try it out**
>
> Osayande Obery Hendricks invites African Americans to undertake 'guerrilla exegesis' of the Bible using blues, soul and jazz music (Hendricks 1994, cited in Sugirtharajah 1999, p. 100). Find a Bible passage you would like to interpret in the light of your own local culture. Think about what art forms are important to you or others around you and begin to explore links between them and your text. In the UK, the art forms could be anything from music performed by local bands and choirs to salsa dance, graffiti or quilting. Don't put limits on what you define as art. Remember that art and culture are also expressed in the physical landscape, e.g. gardening and buildings. What light can gardeners shed on biblical passages on the natural world, for example? Look out for other examples of this. You may find that local artists reflect on biblical topics or themes in a variety of ways.

Gerald West's contextual Bible study resource manual is found here: http://www.hs.unp.ac.za/theology/ujamaa/ (30 January 2006) and click on the link on the left headed: 'Contextual Bible Study'.

Ideological Perspectives

Ideology is not a dirty word, and does not only describe the beliefs of fanatics or extremists! Soulen and Soulen define it as 'a set of attitudes and ideas ... that reflects or shapes understanding (and misunderstandings) of the social and political world, and that serves to justify collective action aimed at preserving or changing it' (2001, p. 84). In this sense, everybody works with an ideology, and it is important that people are aware of the one that shapes their thinking.

Ideological criticism considers three areas in which ideology affects texts: the ideological context(s) in which it was produced, the ideology expressed within it and the ideology of those who read and interpret it (Soulen and Soulen 2001, p. 84). In each of these areas, ideologies affirm and uphold the interests of some at the expense of others. Ideological approaches to the Bible help us to see this, so that we can act in ways that overcome the effects of this distortion. We become more aware of the blind spots in our own perspective and can interpret the Bible in ways that are more respectful of the needs and interests of others. Moreover, this approach encourages us to notice ways in which established methods of interpretation neglect important issues.

Feminist criticism

Chapter 4 encouraged us to think about how gender shapes our experience as a reader. There we also identified aspects of feminist approaches to the Bible. Feminist criticism is an ideological response to the differences created by gender. First, feminist scholars suggest that since the majority of biblical texts were written by and for men, they cannot adequately represent the experience and contribution of women. Second, since most biblical interpretation has been (and is still) done by men, much scholarship ignores, undervalues or distorts the role of women, both in the events described within the biblical narrative and in the contemporary situation. For these reasons, some feminists believe the Bible cannot speak a liberating word to women and should therefore be set aside.

However, most feminist interpreters believe that it is possible to respond to the patriarchal bias of the text in ways that retrieve the Bible's liberating potential for both men and women. They use a range of interpretative tools to help them do this. Feminist historians, for example, use historical-critical, anthropological and archaeological tools to reconstruct the history of activity by women and actions against women in ancient Israel, Judaism and the early church. Similarly feminist literary critics 'uncover androcentric ideologies encoded in biblical texts, to highlight neglected female images of God or neglected stories of women, and to identify women's genres' (Pressler 1996, p. 26). As one example of this approach, feminine images in the Bible, such as Jesus' image of himself as a mother hen (Matt. 23.37) or the image of the spirit of God brooding over creation at the start of Genesis (Gen. 1.2) have gained increasing usage in contemporary Christian prayers and hymns.

Pressler describes feminist criticism as engaged, communal and contextual. As an engaged approach it views biblical interpretation as a political act, particularly conscious of the political situation faced by women in society. In this respect, feminist interpretation is not only interested in the well-being of women, but in the healing and transformation of society as a whole (Pressler in Farmer 1998, pp. 283–4). Sharon Ringe (1998, pp.1–9) offers a similar profile of feminist biblical interpretation, noting how such interpreters read the Bible through the lens of women's experience, challenging the ambivalent authority and power of the Bible in a variety of ways, and staying attentive to the way the gender and social, historical and economic context of interpreters affect what they can – and cannot – see in a text. She concludes:

> Interpretation itself is an active project, undertaken in a particular context, in dialogue with many partners both ancient and modern, and with the pastoral and theological purpose of hearing and sustaining a word of healing and liberation in a hurting world. (Ringe in Newsom and Ringe 1998, p. 9)

Try it out

Look up earlier references to feminist and womanist interpretations of the Bible in Chapters 2 and 4. Jot down some notes about the commitments of this approach.

Then read the advice to wives and husbands in 1 Peter 3.7. Historical criticism enables us to see that the author is seeking to make the best Christian use of conventional marriage arrangements in the late first century CE. To what extent should interpreters today recommend that Christians follow these ancient guidelines?

Social scientific criticism

Social scientific criticism uses the tools and assumptions of the social sciences to understand the social dimension of the Bible more accurately.

The most traditional way of doing this is to retain a historical approach to the text. Social historians seek to build up their understanding of the social world of the texts through a close reading of the text read against the background of information from traditional disciplines such as ancient history, classical studies and archaeology. In this way they build up an informed but limited idea of the social worlds in which the texts were written, edited and used. This social-historical approach to the world of the Bible has much to commend it as a focus, as the work of New Testament scholars such as Abraham J. Malherbe on the Thessalonian letters (1987, 2000) or David Aune on Revelation (1997–8) shows. For example, Malherbe's comparison of Paul's approach to pastoral care with those of other moral teachers of the time shows Paul to be consistently mild and self-giving in a way that moral philosophers would have considered to be dangerously close to compromising their integrity (Malherbe 1987, p. 109).

However, other scholars criticize this approach for being neither social nor historical enough. These scholars use methods borrowed from the social sciences – sociology, cultural anthropology and psychology – to do social-scientific criticism of the Bible. While still remaining interested in history, these approaches read the text through the lens of modern social science and therefore differ from the older social history method by being synchronic. Stephen Barton notes how they take snapshots of the complex web of relationships between social actors in the text, and look for meaning in the 'complex web of culturally determined social systems and patterns of communication' between them (Barton 1995, p. 69).

Sociological critics are interested both in the social background of the text and what it describes, and the social context and location of the initial audience. Greater knowledge of the social context has moved biblical interpreters away from seeing simple parallels between the Bible and their own context. Such critics also ask questions about the social function of the text: for example, does it appear to encourage social conformity or try to resocialize its readers?

Anthropological critics use models drawn from anthropology to study phenomena in the Bible such as social structure, myths, magic or sacrifice. Jerome Neyrey, for example, uses a model developed for studying societies in which witchcraft accusations appear to shed light on Paul's relationships in Galatians, providing new insight into Paul's provocative language in Galatians 3:1, 'You foolish Galatians! Who has bewitched you?'

Fewer critics have used psychological models to interpret the Bible, but Gerd Theissen, a pioneer of sociological approaches, has drawn upon models from three areas of the psychology of religion to interpret Paul's theology (Theissen 1987). The models he uses are: learning theory, psychodynamic models and cognitive models. In his study of Romans 7 and 8, for example, he applies these models successively. Learning theory shows that through Christ Christians can 'unlearn' their anxiety response to the law; psychodynamic theory helps to show how Paul's encounter with Christ enabled him to face repressed conflict and cognitive models show that when Paul understood his inner conflict in a new light, he was able to change (Theissen 1987, pp. 222–75).

Models derived from the social sciences can thus be effective thinking tools as Margaret MacDonald explains:

> they can bring hitherto unconscious levels of thought into awareness; they enlarge our control over data. Models can also facilitate understanding for the reader by clearly identifying the writer's frame of reference and by making it more readily available for criticism. The use of models can lead to greater comprehensiveness when doing interpretations by providing categories and suggesting relations between categories. (MacDonald 1988, p. 26)

They can therefore be very useful for filling gaps in the often limited historical information we have about what life was like, say in the cities and churches of Paul's day. Clearly the success of this approach depends on the appropriateness of the model being used and the amount of data available. Critics of this approach warn that models developed on the basis of social interactions today may be anachronistic. There are also concerns that social scientific approaches do not work well when interpreting narratives that describe unusual or unique events, such as Moses' encounter with God on Sinai or Jesus' resurrection.

There is a further ideological concern. The social sciences are rooted in the Enlightenment view that we should not understand human behaviour, even religious behaviour, with reference to belief in God. John Barton points out that this ideological framework prefers to account for theology and religion as 'the products of other forces and interests, whether the human unconscious (Freud), economic relations and class interest (Marx), the maintenance of society (Durkheim), or the legitimation of patriarchal domination (feminism)' (Barton, 1995, p. 76). While these kinds of ideological challenges are helpful, and often provoke fresh insights, we should be aware that the secular ideological roots of social scientific approaches to the Bible can downplay some issues of prime importance to biblical writers, such as a character's encounter with God.

Social scientific approaches are diverse and controversial, but they have deepened our knowledge of and sensitivity to four social aspects of biblical texts: the material culture (food, clothing, work, institutions), the social history of groups, the social organization of movements and their social worlds (Soulen and Soulen 2001, pp. 177–8). Many biblical scholars draw information from all four of these research areas, without necessarily applying social science methods rigorously. Their use of insights from social scientific approaches is eclectic, intuitive and pragmatic. For most, sociological models are suggestive, rather than analytic tools, and they continue to rely heavily on historical criticism to verify their findings.

For the practical task of biblical interpretation, social scientific approaches offer two other benefits. They remind us that the original authors and readers of the Bible lived in a material world, and so do we. They also remind us that our own experience of reality, including our experience of reading and interpreting the Bible, is socially constructed.

Try it out

Baptism is a central initiation ritual for Christians, and there are a number of descriptions of its significance in Paul's letters, e.g. Romans 6.3–12, 1 Corinthians 6.9–11 and Galatians 3.26–29.

Read one of these passages, noting that social-scientific criticism would bring such questions to it:

- What did this rite look like in action, and what would it communicate to the Roman, Corinthian or Galatian churches?
- What social relations (internal relations, boundaries and the like) was this rite used to promote?
- What interpretation does Paul give to this rite?

- How does the Christian's participation in this rite shape or reinforce his or her experience of everyday life, worldview and priorities?

This exercise is adapted from David de Silva's *Introduction to the New Testament* (2004, p. 631). This textbook contains many useful examples of exegetical methods and a number of worked illustrations of social-scientific readings of New Testament texts.

Deconstruction

The most radical ideological criticism of the Bible is that of deconstruction, a perspective associated with the philosopher and literary critic Jacques Derrida. This approach unsettles and decentres all readings of texts. It shows that there is no such thing as the centre of a text because every centre depends on the margins to exist as a centre. In this way it shows that the margins are as important as the centre, and cannot therefore be ignored. This internal contradiction undermines the coherence of all texts. Those who have seen this realize that the messages conveyed by texts are much less stable than they thought. Texts can be read playfully and subversively.

While some interpreters are unsettled by deconstruction, others welcome it, since it weakens the position of those in power who try to preserve their power by imposing oppressive interpretations of the Bible on others. Segovia comments, 'The process of deconstruction is going on in Third World theologies without using the term; indeed, decolonizing theology is a form of deconstruction' (Segovia in Fabella and Sugirtharajah 2000, p. 67). It alerts readers to the way that the Bible also decentres readers in ways that open them to new discoveries about themselves and God.

Gina Hens-Piazza observes how postmodern approaches to the Bible similarly increase our interest in marginal texts and characters:

As postmodern literary criticism pays attention to the seams, unanswered questions, or cracks in the narrative it often uncovers competing voices, values and centers of power in the story. It raises unaddressed questions lurking in the margins that disrupt the integrity of a unified reading.

> Attention to these contradictory, contestatory, or incongruous elements in texts often leads to interpretations that challenge the prevailing wisdom about a biblical story. In the process we discover how rhetoric is not just artistic or innocent but may participate in the violence of exclusion. (Hens-Piazza 2003, p. 74)

She observes how contemporary literary-critical methods give us greater freedom to choose where to focus our attention. While once we were expected to follow the lead of the narrator or line of the story, now we have the option of ignoring such guidance and linger with the background incidents or minor characters. There are new and important insights to be gained with this shift in our attentions. In recent years, for example, there has been a wealth of popular devotional literature created about minor characters in the Gospel stories, especially women. Through first-person narratives, short dramas or poems, new perspectives and points of contact with these figures have been developed for Christians. Often, the fictional extensions of these biblical characters relate their encounter with Jesus, thus encouraging a devotional response from readers.

Try it out

Read Matthew 21.12–17 and focus on either the children in the temple or the chief priests and scribes. What is their role and perspective in the story? Do you feel drawn to develop a 'background story' for these characters?

Paying attention the margins of a story challenges traditional readings, destabilizing the centre to allow new aspects of the story to emerge. This should not lead us to reject older readings, but rather help us bring together central and marginal perspectives to gain a fuller sense of what a passage is about.

Overall, ideological approaches to the Bible open up spaces for people to read the Bible with their own interests and needs in mind. This includes the many Bible readers who read the Bible with a faith commitment.

Faith Perspectives

The third cluster of committed approaches all view the Bible from the perspective of religious faith. In this section we focus mainly on examples of reading the Bible from an explicitly Christian perspective, and do not include many examples from the Jewish tradition. While Christians view the Bible in many different ways, there is widespread agreement that the Bible plays an essential role in guiding Christian belief and behaviour. Looking at the relationship between Christian understanding and the Bible from the other direction, many Christians would agree with Augustine of Hippo (354–430) that the Bible should be interpreted in the context of Christian commitment and worship. Towards the end of the first book of *On Christian Doctrine* he insists that the purpose of Scripture is to enable people to love God for God's own sake and their neighbours for God's sake. And so he is able to say:

> Whoever, then, thinks that he understands the Holy Scriptures, or any part of them, but puts such an interpretation upon them as does not tend to build up this twofold love of God and our neighbour, does not yet understand them as he ought. (Augustine, *On Christian Doctrine*, 1.36.40)

Augustine suggested that since the Bible was written from a faith perspective which places the love of God and others as the supreme value, it is best understood by readers who share, or wish to share, that perspective. In the following section we look at methods Christians use to interpret the Bible from this perspective. While individuals can practise some of these methods, they are all essentially communal, because Christian faith is held and expressed communally through the Church.

Meditative, prayerful Bible reading

In the city of Santiago de Chile in South America, a group of Christian women have been meeting regularly since 1991 to discuss their faith and their world. Known as the *Con-spirando* collective, they pray, act and reflect together. To 'conspire' is literally to 'breathe-with' and Christians think of their study of the Scriptures as breathing with God. For the women of *Con-spirando*, this breathing together has led them to new ways of worshipping and following God, for example through caring for the earth. For more information, see www.conspirando.cl

Just as most Judeo-Christian spiritual traditions are rooted in Scripture, so most traditional methods of biblical interpretation are rooted in prayer. Ignatius of Loyola's (1491–1556) *Spiritual Exercises*, for example, were designed to help readers enter more deeply and imaginatively into the story of Jesus.

Jewish and Christian readers tend to begin Bible study with an opening prayer. Some traditions understand this opening prayer as a plea for God to guide them to a correct interpretation of the passage. For others, this prayer expresses their commitment to remain open to God as they approach the Scriptures afresh, bringing with them their current questions or concerns.

Try it out

If you do surround your reading or study of the Bible with prayer, think about how this affects your understanding of the text and your relationship with it. What does it 'do'?

Lectio divina is a prayerful and meditative way of reading the Bible that goes back to the earlier days of monastic life in the Christian tradition, and was also practised by early Jewish communities. Hans-Ruedi Weber describes it thus:

> It consists of a daily attempt to listen to God's word within a prescribed biblical text. This happens at regular hours according to a lectionary which covers the whole Bible, so that for example the whole book of Psalms or all four gospels are read consecutively. Sensitivity to resonances from the whole Bible is needed so that the scripture itself interprets the meditated scripture passage and so that God's word heard shapes human thought and life. (Weber 1995, p. 48)

Note that Weber distinguishes between God's word and the biblical text. The two are not directly equated. God's word is heard through a process of prayerful meditation on a Bible passage. Writing about this process often describes it in colourful similes: the reader's thoughts are like bees buzzing around a sacred hive, the pages of the sacred book being read are like rows of a vineyard, and each letter of the text is like a juicy grape to be chewed. These examples come from the glossary to the following website of the Sacred Reading project of the Catholic Parramatta Diocese, New South Wales, Australia: http://ceo-web.parra.catholic.edu.au/re/readroom/sacread/index.html. The site offers a wealth of information on Jewish and Christian methods of sacred reading and guidance on how to use them.

Lectio is not an academic investigation of the Scriptures but a process of encounter with God's word. Thus as a method, it affects the reader's attitude to the text. If we wish to experiment with this approach, we need to adopt a patient, humble and open attitude to the Bible. There is a sense of letting go, even losing control – the reader does not set the agenda but waits on God's word which may be consoling, affirming or demanding. Of course, this leaves the reader vulnerable – particularly to problematic or violent texts. But it can also provide a deep encounter with 'good news'.

> Significantly, for the modern reader *lectio* is a form of surrender, of letting go. God leads the way and sets the agenda; we are never sure where the practice of *lectio* will lead. In a very real sense, we give up control to the sacred text, and only then are we free to enter into that quiet part of the self where we meet God – that place where we can truthfully say whatever needs to be said and listen to Truth in return ... This mingling of prayer and reading that we call *lectio divina* brings us into contract with God, and through the liberating power of the Word of God we begin the journey into wisdom. (O'Donnell 1990, pp. 49–50)

Lectio is part of a wider spiritual process:

- Preparation – Finding a quiet space and becoming more focused and attentive.
- Lectio (reading) – Slowly reading aloud or recalling a passage. Pausing on a phrase or word that seems significant.
- Meditatio (meditation) – Repeating this phrase or word until it is known 'by heart'.
- Oratio (prayer) – Beginning a dialogue with God.

- Contemplatio (contemplation) – Encountering and responding to God in prayer and life.

> **Try it out**
>
> Read a psalm in this way. At the end of the process, reflect on how *lectio* enabled you to know the psalm 'by heart'. Did you find this reading method comfortable or challenging?

Since *lectio* involves repetition and memorizing, it enables the reader to 'bank' phrases and longer scriptural passages in their memory, for contemplation and use throughout the day. *Lectio* was originally an individual exercise as devotees considered the word of God for them in that moment. However, there are also methods of corporate *lectio* where groups hear and reflect on Scripture together.

If this method of reading appeals to you, you may like to look at one of Kathleen Norris' books, such as *The Cloister Walk* (1996), *Amazing Grace* (1998) or *Dakota: A Spiritual Geography* (1993). Kathleen Norris is a journalist and writer who reflects on her faith and life in the context of the Great Plains of North America. During her lengthy stays at a local Benedictine monastery, Norris learned the practice of *lectio* and began to apply it not only to Scripture but also the plains surrounding her. This reminds us that *lectio divina* is a meditative and prayerful approach to listening for God's word, and can include other books and the world around us. The biblical passage becomes a perspective through which these other 'texts' are read, and they in turn serve as a commentary on the passage.

Reading in worship

Readers more naturally follow meditative approaches to the Bible when reading alone. However, when approached with faith, the Bible is best read and interpreted with others. This can happen in a variety of situations, including public worship, church Bible studies or workshops or theological college seminars. Each of these contexts affects how the Bible is heard.

When a passage from the Bible is read in Christian worship it is read in the context of the canon and the Christian faith. We saw in Chapter 2 that there is a close relationship between canonical boundaries and the faith they are intended to uphold. Thus, when a passage is read in church it is heard in relation to other Bible passages which are read on the same occasion and in relation to the Christian faith of the hearers. The reading is normally introduced and/or concluded with a statement which urges listeners to hear the passage as 'the word of the Lord' or 'the holy gospel'. Also, the readings are usually accompanied by a sermon exploring an aspect of the Christian faith, and a summary of the Christian faith, such as a creed or hymn. There may be other associated actions too, such as standing when the Bible is brought into church or read, or burning incense to indicate the holiness of the text being read.

This worship context is intended to help people adopt a receptive attitude to the text out of reverence for God. This can have similar benefits to those noted for *lectio*. On the other hand, it can have the effect of discouraging them from thinking critically about the passage, especially if it is problematic for some hearers. Here is an example from the experience of one of the authors. Every morning while studying at seminary in New York, she met with two or three others to pray. One morning the text for the day was 1 Timothy 2:

> 11 Let a woman learn in silence with full submission. 12 I permit no woman to teach or to have authority over a man; she is to keep silent. 13 For Adam was formed first, then Eve; 14 and Adam was not deceived, but the woman was deceived and became a transgressor. 15 Yet she will be saved through childbearing.

The reader then proclaimed, 'This is the word of the Lord'. But the rest of the group withheld the words, 'Thanks be to God'. There was silence and then laughter. As a community of prayer, the group withheld their consent to these words, which they experienced as damaging. They refused to acquiesce to the text.

This is an example of the way we often draw on other sources of knowledge, such as our own faith experience, when we interpret Scripture. Readers learn to value insights or revelation in their lives as well as through the lives recorded in the Bible. We will consider how we draw together these different sources of knowledge in Chapter 6.

Try it out

There are a number of vindictive prayers in the psalms which are sometimes omitted from use in church worship. Psalms like 58 and 83 are omitted from some lectionaries altogether, while others have the offending verses omitted (see Psalms 59.5–8 and 69.9–10 and 22–28). Yet, such psalms are part of the Bible. Kathleen Farmer points out that, 'these prayers describe the way real people in real situations have felt in the past and may still feel today' (Farmer in Farmer 1998, p. 826). Read one or more of these psalms and consider the benefits and risks of reading them in the context of public worship.

Canonical criticism

There is a close relationship between the ideas of canon and discipleship. We noted in Chapter 2 how the believing community sets the boundaries of the biblical canon. The church and Jewish community see the Bible as a collection of documents which have grown and been collected out of the process of living the life of faith. Therefore, it is in the context of living out the life of faith in the believing community that it is properly interpreted. Brevard Childs' (1979) *Introduction to the Old Testament as Scripture* is the classic statement of this position and an important resource for interpreting the Hebrew Bible from this perspective. His 1985 work *The New Testament as Canon: An introduction* aimed to do the same for the New Testament, but scholars criticized its view of the development of the New Testament and it has been much less influential. Childs describes 'the form and function of the books of the Hebrew Bible in its role as sacred Scripture for Israel' while recognizing that this is the spiritual heritage of Christians too (Childs 1979, p. 16).

When the Bible is interpreted within the context of the canon, interpreters expect it to provide reliable and helpful information about, and even access to, the object of Jewish and Christian faith – God. Theological exegesis looks for information in the text about God, persons specifically related to God, other supernatural beings, divine or sacred history, human redemption by God, human commitment to God, community, ethics and so on (Gorman 2001, pp. 20–1, 130). As we noted in Chapter 3, within the constraints of responsible historical-critical exegesis, such information is considered to be reliable.

When we considered the canon in Chapter 2, we noted that canonical criticism is the critical approach which engages most closely with faith perspectives on the Bible. Without necessarily sharing the faith perspective of worshippers, canonical critics recognize that the books of the Bible were written and collected with the main purpose of forming the faith of believing communities. This is a two-way process – the texts were produced by the communities and the communities were in turn shaped by the texts they produced and used to guide their living.

Canonical critics explore why these texts in particular were collected and ask in what ways they were considered to be authoritative for the faith communities concerned. By asking such historical questions, they are able to rule out some interpretations as possible, but unlikely. Canonical criticism trusts the historical process of canon formation. It recognizes that there are many voices in the Bible but believes when readers listen to all these voices and allow them to converse with one another, theological understanding grows. It believes that the canon contains within itself resources for its interpretation. In Brevard Childs' words, 'the canon provides the arena in which the struggle for understanding takes place' (Childs 1985, p. 15, cited by Calloway 1999, p 147).

Interpretation for discipleship

Committed, contextual biblical interpretation is not just for people conscious of experiencing social or political oppression. Today, more and more readers of the Bible throughout the world are recognizing that an essential component of biblical interpretation is the step by which they identify what the passage is encouraging them to do – and then attempt to do it! Gorman calls this method embodiment or actualization. It asks, 'If readers took the message of this text seriously, how would their lives be different?' (Gorman 2001, pp. 131–3, 203).

While interpretation for discipleship may appear to be simply a western term for contextual interpretation, there are differences. The main contexts which affect interpretation here are the church and the canon. The interpreter's location in the life of the church and the text's location within the canon both affect the scope and focus of acts of interpretation. While other contextual factors are not ignored, in practice they often play only a supporting role. Not surprisingly, interpretation for discipleship often focuses on the spiritual and theological meanings of the text, rather than on its political or social impact.

Recently, western biblical scholars have begun preparing commentaries aimed at fostering discipleship. That is, the explicit purpose of their interpretative work is to help people know and follow God. A recent example of this for the North-American context is the collection of essays entitled *The New Testament: Introducing the way of discipleship* (2002) edited by Wes Howard-Brook and Sharon Ringe. It aims to bridge the gap between conventional introductions to the New Testament and the real-life questions of people's lives, and to make a 'link between the struggles of our ancestors and our own struggles; between the challenge of discipleship in Jesus' time, and in our own' (Howard-Brook and Ringe 2002, p. ix).

These scholars make their social location, ideological commitments and exegetical purposes explicit. This helps to ground and reveal the limits of their acts of interpretation. They also all make clear that they need the help of others in the believing community to live out their ideological and faith commitments. Refreshingly, for readers used to seeing scholars maintain a safe distance from the life of the church, these scholars even try to identify ways that the church can help them do this.

For example, Howard-Brook concludes his chapter on Revelation with the statement: 'Without a small faith community in which to attempt experiments in alternative economics, I would feel lost' (2002, p. 206). Katherine

Grieb's commitment to her role as an ecclesial Scripture interpreter enables her to stay with some of the deutero-Pauline texts with which she fundamentally disagrees:

> I am called as an interpreter of the New Testament *for the church*, to honour that tension and to stay in conversation with others, precious in the sight of God, with whom I disagree. I am also called to stay 'in conversation' with these ancient writers, who either read the historical Paul very differently than I do, or, as I think, were so troubled by Paul that they found it necessary to correct his theology at several points (particularly his political theology) by writing letters in his name. (Grieb in Howard-Brook and Ringe 2002, p. 166 her italics)

What is helpful to us is to see just how complex this interpretative strategy can be. Because the Gospel of Luke itself makes compromises with its context, Sharon Ringe finds herself in an ambivalent relationship towards it. She struggles to balance a range of factors: her privileged social and economic position, her position as a woman in solidarity with those on the margins, and the dangerous compromises away from the radicality of the gospel which she identifies in Luke's Gospel itself (Ringe in Howard-Brook and Ringe, 2002, p. 79).

These tensions are not a bad thing. They are the consequence of faith perspectives incorporating a variety of viewpoints: both the canon and the believing community contain a variety of viewpoints. Responsible interpretation requires ongoing conversation between them. While some of the committed approaches to interpretation are content to allow these conversations to remain within the canon or within the believing communities, most insist that other conversation partners are necessary.

Interactive group Bible studies are one of the ways the Bible can be interpreted corporately, relationally and in dialogue with other interests. Such approaches can be quite simple, for example memorizing and retelling Bible narratives or doing *lectio divina* together in a busy town centre. Other approaches can be more complex: exploring biblical themes in contemporary art, writing letters to biblical characters or imagining new incidents in biblical narratives. By pressing participants to draw, use memory and imagination to interact with the Bible, such approaches help them to see for themselves that the Bible is a product of memory, experience, imagination and faith. It also often leads participants to transforming personal insights. The best resource book for this is Hans-Ruedi Weber's (1995) *The Book that Reads Me*, which offers a rich collection of examples.

Using commentaries

In the final section of this chapter, we look at the use of commentaries to aid interpretation. There is a reason why this topic has been deferred to now: if consulted too early, commentaries impair our ability to listen to the Bible for ourselves. They can intimidate us by their scholarly language and learning, influence us to view the text with their biases, disappoint us by ignoring what we think is important, drown out the soft voices within the text which are straining to be heard, particularly the voices of those on the social margins, and so on. In a nutshell, they can make us forget the very questions we brought to the text to find answers. We need to remember that commentaries should be used to support rather than direct our own interpretative investigation.

When we have arrived at our own provisional understanding of a passage, it is time to test and refine this through conversation with others. Commentaries can provide some of these conversation partners. Commentaries, like friends, need to be chosen wisely. Our choices will be based on our own changing circumstances and needs. This means that there is no answer to the question, 'What is a good commentary on such and such a book?' without also considering, 'Good for whom?' and 'Good for what purpose?'

Guidance for choosing a commentary

When looking for commentaries to consult, we should start by considering our own experience. Have we used commentaries before? If so, what did we use them for, and which ones did we find to be most helpful for that purpose? If we have had commentaries on our bookshelves for many years, but have hardly looked at them, it may be worth asking ourselves why this is and whether they are likely to be much help now. There are so many modern commentaries available that it is quite unnecessary (and unwise for beginners) to struggle with difficult or outdated commentaries. There is a place for classic commentaries from the past, but guidance and experience will be needed to know which these are.

Next we consider what new purposes we might have for consulting commentaries. If we think of the tools introduced in this book, we will be aware that we need commentaries to provide some basic information about the book from which our chosen passage comes, and a very wide range of detailed information. Most commentaries provide the basic historical and literary information we need to orientate ourselves, e.g. the genre of the book, where it was written, by whom, when, to/for whom on the one hand, and its shape and major subdivisions on the other. However, even on the basics, commentators will differ, so more than one needs to be consulted.

As far as detailed information is concerned, no single commentary, no matter how large, will provide all the information we need. So we need to choose commentaries that focus on our area of interest. We will be guided in our search by knowing as much as possible about the author(s) of the commentary: their age, gender, nationality, ethnicity, vocation, research interests, denominational or religious affiliation, and so on, remembering that all commentaries are products of earlier conversations with other interpreters. So, we should choose commentaries that seem to be engaged in a conversation that is interesting to us. When approaching a topic or biblical book for the first time, it is wise to look for that interaction with the scholarly consensus, rather than those arguing for new or untested views.

We also need to consider our own current level of technical skills. For example, if we have some knowledge of classical Hebrew or *koine* Greek, then commentaries that refer to the original languages will be useful. If we don't, we will want to be assured that the author knows the original language of the passage, and is sensitive to the needs of readers who do not. Real experts are usually able to explain complex matters simply, and it is usually safe to avoid authors who seem over complex.

Some commentaries, e.g. those in the *Bible Speaks Today* series published by IVP, are more expositions than commentaries. Frequently, such expositions have been written up on the basis of series of sermons or Bible readings given in a particular church context. If the expositor has taken the trouble to be a thorough interpreter, and if the context for which the expositions were prepared is similar to the one we are engaging with, then such interpretations may offer us useful guidance. However, we should use such expositions with caution.

Remember that people's needs differ. Here are some questions we might ask when we consider using a commentary for a particular interpretative task:

- Is it easy to use?
- Does the introduction help us see the shape of the text and the key theological issues?
- Is it written with reference to the original language(s)?
- Does it make good use of appropriate exegetical tools?
- Does it make connections with issues in contemporary life?
- Does it take a committed approach: political, theological, denominational, etc.? If so, what? If not, what ideological commitments is the author concealing?

Published guides to commentaries

Despite the attraction of owning a set of books with matching covers, we should not buy complete sets or series, unless we have already found a number of volumes in the series very useful. Commentaries in series are usually written by different authors, and so vary in quality. It is worth knowing the general character of a particular commentary series, as we will find some series useful and others unhelpful at whatever stage we are in our work of interpretation. Soulen and Soulen (2001, pp. 36–7) offer a brief description of some of the major series.

Further help with the choosing of commentaries can be found in larger guides to commentaries. These books about modern books about ancient biblical books also need to be interpreted with care. We should take particular note of the purposes and orientation of the authors of these guides.

Most of those listed below are by evangelical Christians who have relatively conservative views of the inspiration of the Bible (limited verbal inspiration or non-textual inspiration; see Chapter 2). However, they are also written by scholars who understand the complexity of the exegetical and hermeneutical task faced by commentators. At times these authors say, in effect, 'This is a great commentary with a lot to teach us, even though the author is wrong in his/her view about ... '. Overall, these guides are useful both in describing the character of series as a whole and, especially, in identifying which are particularly good volumes within each series, as well as classics.

The best single-volume guide to books which aid the study of the Bible is Bauer's *An Annotated Guide to Biblical Resources for Ministry* (2003). This is particularly useful as it also provides guidance on other important study aids such as: concordances, word studies, lexicons, introductions, etc. Longman III provides a useful guide to Old Testament commentaries in *Old Testament Commentary Survey* (2003) and Carson's *New Testament Commentary Survey* (1993) is informed but now dated. One useful online resource is the Grove *Biblical Studies Bulletin*. To locate this go to the Grove homepage at http://www.grovebooks.co.uk/index.htm and then to the Biblical Studies Bulletin section. Each issue includes a guide to commentaries on a particular biblical book by evangelical scholars and church leaders.

Finally, we should not just find and stick to our favourite authors but remember that it is also important to look at commentaries written from a perspective different from our own, and with different commitments. These help us to see where our blind spots or prejudices are and widen our vision.

6

Enabling Dialogue with the Text

Introduction

When we have a conversation with someone else, there are certain rules we follow. We have to make time available for the conversation, listen carefully to what the other person says so we can respond appropriately and be able to express our own views. We will usually find some common ground as well as some differences of opinion. Good dialogue also requires us to be honest about our views but open to change. And in any conversation, someone has the last word, which either opens up further dialogue or closes it down.

In this chapter we explore our dialogue with the Bible. How can we accurately hear what the Bible says, particularly when it speaks with several voices? How do we bring our experience into the conversation? And who should have the last word? We have already done much of the preparatory work for this penultimate stage in our interpretative process. In Chapter 3, we explored the tools at our disposal for examining the Bible and taking account of a passage's shape, context and formation. We then considered how we talk about ourselves and our context honestly (Chapter 4) as well as the impact our commitments make to our reading (Chapter 5). We are now ready to bring all these elements together and consider the various hermeneutical approaches we might use.

For most Christians and Jews, the Bible takes on the role of the primary dialogue partner. Its authoritative status in these communities means that its contribution to any conversation is regarded as trustworthy and of significance. For such readers, remembering how the Bible has offered guidance and hope in their own lives and the lives of their community of faith in the past, gives them reason to continue to place their trust in the Bible. However, as we saw in Chapter 2, many other readers see the Bible differently. For them, the Bible is just one conversation partner and must take its turn alongside their life experience and other knowledge such as scientific theory or ideological criticism.

Whether we prioritize the text or our experience, we should note that neither can be relied on to 'keep to the script'. The range of voices, contexts and theological or ideological positions represented across the Bible makes it difficult to fix what the Bible teaches about any theological or ethical issue. Equally, readers who prioritize their lived experience rather than the experience reflected in the Bible, have to take account of how this changes over time.

Because of the fluid nature of both reader and text, we have already acknowledged that questions about the meaning of a biblical passage can only be answered for a particular time and place. The outcome of the dialogue will change depending on who is involved in the conversation. We should therefore be cautious of any attempt to establish a universally authoritative interpretation of a passage. The Bible always has more to add to the discussion, as do we as readers. Walter Brueggemann (1997b, p. 59) encourages readers to respect the density of the biblical text and its contexts of formation and reception and warns against what he calls 'thin' kinds of scholarship (Brueggemann 1997b, p. 61), interpretations that stay at the surface of the text.

The aim of this chapter is to explore how we can engage in fruitful dialogue with the Bible, whatever our understanding of its authority. We can never read the Bible without our reading being influenced in some way by our own life experience and as we noted in Chapter 4, it is important to acknowledge this so that it enriches our study rather than obstructing it. How then do we hold those insights from our experience and those that emerge from the text in creative tension? What kind of working relationship should we try to create?

Let us explore these introductory observations by looking at a range of approaches to John 10.14 in which the evangelist records Jesus' claim, 'I am the good shepherd.' If we were to read the passage against the background of the whole canon, we would note various connections between this verse and other texts. It recalls the opening line of Psalm 23, 'The Lord is my shepherd; I shall not want' suggesting that the writer of John saw Jesus as acting out God's role on earth. The passage also alludes to the judgement of Ezekiel on certain leaders of Israel who are characterized as careless shepherds who do not care for the flock or search for lost sheep (Ezek. 43). Finally, the passage in John could be regarded as an enacted version of the parable of the lost sheep (Luke 15.1–7).

If we read from a secular perspective, or as someone of a different faith than Christianity, we will inevitably struggle with biblical claims such as the one Jesus makes about his status in John 10.14, even if we accept the artistic value of a passage or its historical accuracy or social insights. If we are Christian readers, however, we might find great comfort in this verse, observing how Jesus' bold claim is supported by his ministry of care and guidance recorded in the four Gospels. The words and deeds of Jesus would confirm for us that Jesus is a righteous leader who will guide and care for us, keep us from harm and bring us to safety. In this way we would interpret the text by exploring the wider biblical narrative and with reference to our own faith experience.

This kind of devotional interpretation makes a single step from Jesus' claim to the reader's own journey of discipleship, with the reader perhaps thinking: 'Jesus is the good shepherd who promises to provide for his followers, therefore I should follow him.' But, historical criticism teaches us that our access to Jesus is mediated by the evangelists and their communities. Therefore, we might want to take a more cautious approach, first exploring the situation and beliefs of the Johannine community, using historical and sociological tools to understand its struggle with the leaders of the Jewish synagogues and their consequent search for new leadership models. Such an approach to the text suggests the focus of the passage is about choosing which leaders to follow and would lead us to consider the competing claims for allegiance we face in our own lives and how we decide whom to trust.

What happens to our interpretation of this verse if we introduce our own experience into the conversation? We could reflect on our own role as leaders or followers, thinking about the characteristics we value in a leader and how we develop our own leadership skills. We might also want to explore what kind of leader Jesus was, and consider whether a shepherd who would die for his sheep (John 10.15) is an appropriate role model today.

Finally, as we have already noted, the lived commitments of some readers will lead them to read the Bible with caution. This verse may therefore cause us to question the notion of a good shepherd. Is the shepherd really good for the sheep? Or is he only good in the eyes of the farmer who profits from the wool and will eventually kill and eat the sheep or their lambs? While noting such cautions, looking at the impact history of this verse, we would note that it has tended to function as an encouragement to readers who are comforted by the image of the good shepherd and encouraged to follow Jesus, trusting in his promise to provide good things.

This example illustrates how we can bring together exegetical tools, our experience and social analysis to shape our interpretation of a passage. In the rest of this chapter, we will explore this process in more detail and try to draw together the resources we have built up in previous chapters.

As we have seen throughout this book, the Bible is a complex work with a mixed history of interpretation. Inevitably in this chapter on hermeneutical methods, we will tend to focus on more problematic or contentious passages, but of course the Bible contains many texts that do not present difficulties to most readers. As readers, we all have different experiences of the Bible and some of us will wrestle at greater length with our interpretations. Whether we find reading the Bible a positive experience or something we struggle with, identifying our interpretative method will help us in our task.

A direct relationship between text and reader

Many readers of the Bible see a direct relationship between the teaching of the Bible and their response, with little need for any kind of interpretation. Certainly, there are some passages within the Bible that seem quite straightforward to us when we read them. These include moral instructions (e.g. 'You shall not steal' (Exod. 20.15), and encouragement to imitate model characters (e.g. Abraham and Sarah are held up as an examples of faith in Heb. 11.8–12).

Try it out

Read Luke 2.25–40, the story of Simeon's and Anna's encounters with the baby Jesus. Simeon and Anna are remembered within the church as wise and faithful people whose patience was rewarded. How does the passage portray them? Which of their characteristics would you want to display in your own life?

From the earliest times, Christians have been encouraged to become Christ-like, with Paul urging 'Let the same mind be in you that was in Christ Jesus' (Phil. 2.5). Thomas à Kempis' spiritual classic *The Imitation of Christ*, written around 1400 CE, encourages readers to meditate on the life and teaching of Christ and influenced Christian approaches to the Bible. Reading the Bible to learn how to follow Jesus is a well-established and valid approach for many Christians. In a modern take on this ancient practice, some Christians wear wrist-straps printed with the letters WWJD that stand for 'What Would Jesus Do?' a reminder to the wearer to act as Jesus would in any situation. The source of the phrase is Charles Sheldon's story *In His Steps* (1896). This method of reflection on the Bible extends beyond personal behaviour into social and political engagement, e.g. a placard at a London *Stop the War* march in 2003 asked, 'Who Would Jesus Bomb?' But as Scott Spencer's study, *What* Did *Jesus Do? Gospel profiles of Jesus' personal conduct* (2003) reminds us, we have no direct access to Jesus' actions, only what the Gospels portray. As with any approach, we need to proceed carefully, using the relevant exegetical tools to ensure our interpretations are accurate and responsible.

Take, for example, the belief that Jesus encourages followers to 'turn the other cheek'. This seemingly straightforward command still needs to be interpreted in relation to the religious, social and political context in which it was given.

Try it out

Read Matthew 5.38–42 and think about Jesus' words and their application today.

Walter Wink's interpretation of Matthew 5.38–42 demonstrates the importance of knowing about Jesus' context as well as his words. While Jesus' command to turn the other cheek has often been understood as encouraging passive acquiescence to evil, Wink suggests Jesus was instead advocating non-violent resistance of the Roman forces. Wink points out that to turn the left cheek towards the social superior who had just slapped the right cheek was a way of resisting the intended humiliation. The superior cannot respond by hitting with the left hand (since it is unclean) but cannot easily give a backward slap onto the left cheek with the right hand either so would only be able to punch the left cheek. But since only people of equal standing punched each other, this would remove the humiliating nature of the act – although not the physical hurt (Wink 1992, pp. 175–84). This example indicates the potential pitfalls of making direct correlations between the Bible and our own situation if the original social context is not properly understood.

Like individual readers who apply biblical teaching directly to their own situation, some communities also draw a close correlation between their situation and situations within the Bible. Some vernacular approaches that we looked at in Chapter 5 do this. To take a further example, many Rastafarians, recalling the transatlantic slave trade, identify their community's experience with that of the Israelites taken into captivity in Babylon. In reggae music and other Rastafari cultural expressions, 'Babylon' is used to indicate America and also Britain; nations people of African origin were taken to by force and where they still suffer racism. There are many biblical allusions in reggae music connecting experience and text, e.g. Bob Marley's song 'Survival' refers to Daniel 3 and the survival of Shadrach, Meshach and Abednego who were thrown into the fiery furnace but 'never get burn'.

Try it out

Listen to one or two reggae tracks (or another music genre that frequently refers to the Bible, such as blues, gospel or hip hop) and listen out for biblical metaphors. What are the benefits and problems of using biblical themes, characters or situations to describe current realities? How does this approach modify your understanding of the original biblical reference?

For further biblical references in reggae music see: http://homepage. ntlworld.com/davebulow/wow/index.htm

The biblical themes of exodus, exile and redemption that reflect foundational events for the Jewish and Christian community are often used in this way. They signify significant moments for Jews and Christians but have also gathered new meanings in different contexts. Because of their depth and range, they can been used to explore numerous situations as the relationship between the Bible and interpretative context can be less obvious or direct. Social commentators who make use of these themes tend not to indicate a clear match but rather use them to hint at a relationship of some kind between the two situations and thus highlight aspects of the contemporary experience. In *Cadences of Home: Preaching among exiles* (1997a), for example, Walter Brueggemann proposes exile as a metaphor for the experience of the church in the USA. He does not propose that the situation of the American church is exactly parallel to that of the Israelite exiles in Babylon centuries before, but rather suggests that for much of America the church is no longer at the centre of cultural life, and Christians often find their beliefs at odds with the dominant consumer culture. Thus they experience a social and moral exile rather than a geographical one.

A correspondence of relationships

In Chapter 5, we looked at how interest in the social background of the Bible and the application of social scientific tools have thrown new light on the situation in which different biblical writings arose. The gap between the worlds described in the Bible and contemporary realities, leads the Brazilian theologian Clodovis Boff to challenge the idea that we can read appropriate actions or responses to our own situation directly from the biblical texts. In his book *Theology and Praxis: Epistemological foundations* (1987), he describes the approach we looked at in the previous section as the 'correspondence of terms', in which the reader sees a direct parallel between the biblical situation and their own context. Boff feels this method drew oversimplistic parallels between biblical contexts such as the exodus and his context of political and economic conflict in Latin America, e.g. in a picture of the massacre of the innocents drawn by members of the Solentiname community (referred to in Chapter 2). Herod's army is replaced with soldiers in the uniform of the Nicaraguan dictator Somoza (Rowland and Corner 1990, p. 55). The correspondence of terms method ignores the fact that the biblical texts reflect layers of contexts, not just the context they claim to describe.

Thus Boff develops the method he calls the 'correspondence of relationships'. This approach notes the layered nature of biblical texts and how they reflect the situation from which they emerged as well as the situation they claim to describe. It takes a lead from how biblical writers adapted earlier events and traditions and applied them creatively to their own situation. By observing how the biblical texts seek to answer the questions of their own day, this method enables the text to be applied creatively and frees it to offer appropriate guidance to readers today. Boff's method is summarized in the following way:

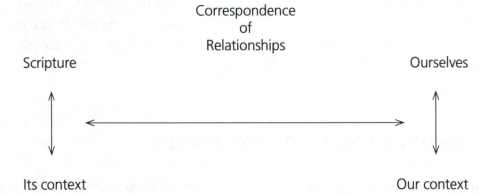

Try it out

Read Jeremiah 32.1–15 in which the prophet Jeremiah is ordered by God to take ownership of a plot of land. Think about what buying a piece of land today could signify, e.g. a sign of increased wealth, a way of preventing further buildings obscuring the view, space for a large animal such as a horse. Next think about what land signifies in the Hebrew Bible: Who owns the land? What is its relationship to the people? In the final verse of the section, Jeremiah's action is revealed as a sign of hope: 'For thus says the Lord of hosts, the God of Israel: Houses and fields and vineyards shall again be bought in this land.' Buying a piece of land today might not signify hope, but what other actions would be seen as 'hopeful' in your context?

The correspondence of relationships approach encourages a flexible method of engagement with the text. Boff observes:

We need not, then, look for formulas to 'copy' or techniques to 'apply,' from scripture. What scripture will offer us are rather something like orientations, models, types, directives, principles, inspirations – elements permitting us to acquire, on our own initiative, a 'hermeneutical competence,' and thus the capacity to judge – on our own initiative, in our own right – 'according to the mind of Christ,' or 'according to the Spirit,' the new, unpredictable situations with which we are continually confronted. The Christian writings offer us not a what, but a how – a manner, a style, a spirit. (Boff 1987, p. 149)

Boff's method is based on an ideological commitment to liberation for the poor. It assumes the Bible advocates liberation as well as entrusting readers to make good judgements about the text and how to apply it to their situation. Boff's encouragement to the reader to make their interpretation according to the mind of Christ relies on an accurate understanding of how Jesus or the early Christians responded to their situation, and as we have seen, this requires close analysis of the social context of the New Testament.

Selecting the best hermeneutical key

The previous two sections of this chapter demonstrated how all interpreters use some sort of hermeneutical key, a principle that guides their dialogue with the text. So far we have considered the interpretative key of imitation and Boff's method that relied on a commitment to liberation as well as consideration of the context of the biblical text. Hermeneutical keys arbitrate over tensions within the Bible, or between disputed interpretations of a passage, or the claims of the text and the reader's own experience. We have already made reference to most of the hermeneutical principles used by readers of the Bible but, at this stage in the book, it may be helpful to have an overview of the various interpretative keys. They fall into three broad areas:

Hermeneutical keys based on the Bible
- Reading the biblical canon as a whole – canonical approach (Chapters 2 and 5)
- Giving priority to some part of the Bible (Chapter 2):
  - the Torah
  - the Gospels
  - or any other form of 'canon within the canon'
- Identifying core teachings or principles
- Reading from the margins – a hermeneutic of suspicion (Chapter 2)

Hermeneutical keys based on faith beliefs
- Foundational events:
  - the Exodus
  - the Christ event or incarnation – Christological approaches
- Theological doctrines or creeds (Chapter 4)
- A faith community's tradition of interpretation (Chapter 5)

Hermeneutical keys based on the reader and their context
- Experience, needs and commitments of a particular community (Chapter 4)
- Other texts and cultural resources (Chapter 4)

The first set of keys represent approaches that encourage dialogue within the text. The other two enable dialogue between text and context. Since we have already considered at length some of these approaches, the following paragraphs focus on those methods that have not yet received much attention.

Hermeneutical keys based on the Bible

In Chapter 2, we looked at the formation and authority of the canon. While some interpreters always try to read individual passages in the context of the canon as a whole, others regard certain sections of the Bible as more authoritative than the rest. The primary example of this approach is the priority given to the Torah in the Jewish tradition and the Gospels in the church. By privileging certain books or themes within the Bible, interpreters are able to judge between diverse teachings.

A canon within the canon

Beyond the identification of either the Torah or the Gospels as the primary texts within the Bible that happens in most Jewish and Christian contexts, various theological factions throughout history have formed their own 'canon within the canon'. These selected canons tend to include teaching that promotes the particular theological or social beliefs of the group. Ernst Käsemann, for example, proposed a 'higher canon' composed of the Gospels and certain Pauline letters such as Romans that were believed to highlight the principle of justification by faith. Some feminist scholars develop their own canon, selecting texts that promote women's well-being. Of course, any such selective approach to the Bible is a form of Marcionism (named after the second-century CE theologian Marcion, whose rejection of the Hebrew Bible is considered in Chapter 2) and, as the following example demonstrates, often fails to resolve interpretative conflict.

Néstor Míguez describes how radical Christian communities in Latin America initially relied on a selection of biblical texts: Exodus, parts of the deuteronomistic history, prophets such as Amos, the synoptic Gospels, the beginning of Acts, James and Revelation. These texts were believed to speak most directly to the Latin America situation. But soon liberation theologians realized, 'It was not enough to quote a handful of favoring passages or create a verse artillery for argument. The "enemy" could do that just as well. A new way of dealing with the whole Bible was needed' (Míguez 2004, p. 9). In response, the liberationist movement shifted 'from a "liberationist canon" to a "canonical liberation"' (Míguez 2004, p. 9). Only by drawing upon the whole canon were liberation theologians able to respond to their critics.

Themes and movements within the canon

Retaining the whole of the Bible instead of keeping to a narrow selection enables us to read texts together and use them to interpret each other. However, we still have to make a judgement between different texts, often based on an understanding of the central message of the Bible. One common approach is to identify a unifying movement or dominant theme within the scriptural narrative. To some extent, all readers of the Bible do this in an attempt to impose some sort of order on the wide-ranging material before them, although each reader may highlight a different core message or movement within the text. We should note, however, that some readers question the existence of an overall pattern or narrative that unites the canonical material, believing that the diversity of the Bible has inherent value since it keeps open the arena of debate.

To explore this approach, we turn to one scholar's attempt to identify a particular movement running throughout the Bible that can then function as an interpretative key. American feminist Rosemary Radford Ruether suggests the Bible itself contains 'resources for the critique of patriarchy and of the religious sanctification of patriarchy' (Ruether 1983, p. 23). She describes these as 'critical prophetic principles' and claims normative status for them. Ruether outlines four themes of the prophetic-liberating tradition of the Bible:

> (1) God's defense and vindication of the oppressed; (2) the critique of the dominant systems of power and their powerholders; (3) the vision of a new age to come in which the present system of injustice is overcome and God's intended reign of peace and justice is installed in history; and (4) finally, the critique of ideology, or of religion, since ideology in this context is primarily religious. (Ruether 1983, p. 24)

Ruether goes on to illustrate the centrality of these themes in the prophets and the synoptic Gospels, for example Amos' critique of cultic worship. She also points out how this prophetic strand acts as an internal critique, 'through which the biblical tradition constantly reevaluates, in new contexts, what is truly the liberating Word of God, over against both the sinful deformations of contemporary society and also the limitations of past biblical traditions' (Ruether 1985, p. 117).

Ruether sees this constant reassessment and search for liberation continuing beyond the Bible into social movements throughout history, suggesting that the biblical principle of prophetic liberation works with the feminist critique to bring about social change. For this reason, the Bible must be read with an eye to the future coming of God's kingdom – or eschatologically, in order that it might offer liberation to groups beyond those liberated by the biblical writers (e.g. women). In summary, Ruether promotes a strand of tradition that can be used to judge the whole of the Bible. For Ruether, these liberative teachings are her 'trump card' that always takes priority over contrary texts or dissident readings.

To offer a worked example of this kind of approach, we turn to Numbers 35 and consider how reading it in the light of a wider movement within the Torah critiques violent interpretations of the individual passage.

Try it out

Read Numbers 35 and note how violence is presented within the chapter. What forms of violence are recorded and how are they regarded? Who is responsible for the different acts of violence? Does God either commend or denounce the violence?

Violence pervades the whole of Numbers 35 and as readers in a still violent world we may question whether the chapter offers us any usable strategies for responding to violence. At first glance, it appears to advocates an eye-for-an-eye method of dealing with murderers which is bound up with notions of moral purity:

You shall not pollute the land in which you live; for blood pollutes the land, and no expiation can be made for the land, for the blood that is shed in it, except by the blood of the one who shed it. You shall not defile the land in which you live, in which I also dwell; for I the Lord dwell among the Israelites. (Num. 35.33–34)

If we believe that retributive justice is the main theme of the Bible, we would be content to conclude our interpretation at this point, noting the need to take responsibility for our actions and be punished accordingly. However, if we think the Bible's overall thrust is more focused on grace and forgiveness, we would need to set this passage in a wider context and explore other ways of understanding these demands. Where else in the Torah does the land respond to blood being spilt?

Try it out

Now read Genesis 4.8–16, 25–26.

How does God respond to the cry of the earth in this passage? How is Abel's death redeemed? Look at both the treatment of Cain and the response of Eve.

By reading Numbers 35 alongside Genesis 4, we discover other methods of responding to bloodshed. Even though Abel's blood pollutes the earth, further blood is not required to restore order, unlike the law outlined in Numbers 35. God does not demand the death of Cain and, although banished, Cain leaves with a mark of protection on him. Moreover, Abel's death is redeemed by the birth of a third child to Eve rather than by another death. Brigitte Kahl notes, 'Eve's naming of Seth takes up the cry of Abel's blood, out of the mouth of the earth. It restores justice ... purifies and decontaminates what has been the source of curse and paralyzed fertility' (Kahl 2001, pp. 66–7). In this reading love, not vengeance, cries out from the earth. Reading Numbers as part of the Torah and using a hermeneutical key that identifies the dominant teaching of the Bible as a proclamation of God's grace opens up the possibility of other readings.

A hermeneutic of suspicion

Towards the end of Chapter 2, we saw how some readers of the Bible prefer to begin at the margins of a story or with texts that have tended to be ignored. They do this because they are suspicious of the story as it has traditionally been told and return to the text to discover the other sides to the story. Such approaches show that it is possible to stay attentive to the text, searching for what is hidden in the shadows, looking for clues left in the silences. They may also include looking beyond the text for other accounts of the described events that might challenge the biblical writer or editor's interpretation.

Feminist interpretations often come to the text with questions about how the text has traditionally been understood, and as Chapter 5 noted, regard biblical interpretation as a political act. One of the most influential feminist biblical scholars, Elizabeth Schüssler Fiorenza has promoted this type of approach. She outlines a fourfold hermeneutic that takes suspicion as its necessary starting point (Fiorenza 1984b). She suggests that suspicion of a biblical text, which has been written and interpreted predominantly by men and used throughout history to marginalize women, is a vital starting point for feminist readers. The second step is one of remembrance, as the reader seeks out the lost and hidden stories of women in the Bible. This leads the reader to the third step of proclaiming a new, fuller witness. Finally this process enables 'creative actualization', as readers realize the liberating potential of their imagination once they begin to read between the lines.

Hermeneutical keys based on Christian belief

The alternative to looking within the Bible for our interpretative key is to look beyond the text for such principles. We have already looked at a number of examples of how other texts, cultural traditions or ideological commitments are brought into dialogue with the Bible. In this section, we will look at examples of when these resources are given priority in the interpretative method.

Selecting an external interpretative principle requires us to be alert to how we might attempt to harmonize the text and external resources, denying the critique they may present to each other. For instance, we noted in Chapter 4 how church doctrines have often been used as a lens through which to read the Bible, and on occasions this has led to Christian theology being imposed on the text rather than emerging from it.

Christological readings

Christian theologians such as the German scholar Karl Barth (1886–1968) argue that Christ should always be at the centre of any attempt to interpret the Bible. For Christians, the incarnation is the central event in history and thus the key to understanding everything else. Reading the Bible through the lens of Christ enables the Christian reader to distinguish between conflicting texts and to keep focused on the core teachings of the gospel. Christological approaches may focus on the salvific event of Christ's life, death and resurrection, or on the ministry and teaching of Jesus.

Although christological readings use an internal interpretative key (the New Testament's witness to Christ), they are dependent nonetheless on the interpretation of the biblical story of Jesus by the church and therefore rely on this as an external principle. The following paragraphs outline various christological approaches to the Bible.

Following Marcion, some Christians effectively ignore the Hebrew Bible, believing the coming of Christ removed the need for these texts. Although few Christians today formally argue for a truncated canon consisting only of the New Testament, the lack of attention and care paid to the Hebrew Bible (e.g. the tendency to preach mainly on New Testament texts in church) indicates how such attitudes are widespread in practice.

Other Christian readers use typological approaches that lead them to see in the Hebrew Bible hidden meanings that reveal Christ and the church. The Hebrew scriptures are believed to have a double meaning, the primary meaning bound to the context of the passage and a second, Christian meaning that is regarded as more important. This approach is present in the New Testament itself, e.g. Romans 5.14: 'Yet death exercised dominion from Adam to Moses, even over those whose sins were not like the transgression of Adam, who is a type of the one who was to come.'

Typology was popular in the early church and medieval period when many Christians used it to see Christ signified in the Hebrew Bible. For example, early Christians interpreted certain motifs within the Joseph narrative to signify Christ and the church: grain and a wine cup; the tree on which a person is hung; periods of three days; descending into a well or into the depths of prison. One of the benefits of typological approaches was their impact on the visual arts as painters brought into dialogue different scenes and characters from both testaments, e.g. the medieval Trier Gospel from Germany includes an image of the baptism of Christ paired with an image of Noah in the ark. (You can see this image on the website of the Centre for Medieval Studies at the Central European University in Budapest: http://www.ceu. hu/medstud/basiliscus/Trier-DS0001.htm)

Typological approaches help keep the Hebrew Bible in the life of the church and prevent Christians from discarding it in favour of the New Testament.

The obvious problem with typological approaches is that they neglect the literal meaning of a text. Therefore, Christians who use a typological approach should always take account of the original meaning of text. The Vatican's document *The Interpretation of the Bible in the Church* (The Pontifical Biblical Commission 1993, cited in Houlden 1995), for example, encourages Catholics to seek out the literal sense of the text, with careful reference to the different types of literary genres in the Bible and the different ways they express truths, as well as the original historical context of the text. This meaning should always be held alongside the insights that emerge through Christian reading. A notable example is how a Christian might understand ancient prophecies being fulfilled with the coming of Christ (as the Gospel writers propose in the infancy and passion narratives). The Vatican teaches that such interpretations of the Hebrew Bible should be understood in continuity with the original literal meaning of the text, noting:

Assumed into the proclamation of the Gospel, they [the books of the Hebrew Bible] acquire and display their full meaning in the 'mystery of Christ' (Ephesians 3.4); they shed light upon multiple aspects of this mystery, while in turn being illuminated by it themselves. (Houlden 1995, p. 73)

Canonical scholars from the Christian tradition also argue that the whole canon witnesses to Jesus but advocate a more developed method of interpreting the Hebrew Bible than a typological one. Brevard Childs argues that if Jews read the Hebrew Bible, Christians read the Old Testament, making clear that Christians always read both testaments together. Childs' approach does not require the reader to reject Jewish understandings but rather he encourages Christians to hold both readings together in a coherent fashion (Brueggemann 1997b, p. 91). Similarly, the Vatican urges Christians, 'to keep unceasingly in mind that, according to the New Testament, the Jews remain "beloved" of God, "since the gifts and callings of God are irrevocable" (Romans 11.28–29)' (Houlden 1995, p. 85).

> ### Try it out
>
> Read Isaiah 52.13–53.12. If you are a Christian reader, think about how your Christian beliefs and the use of this passage in the life of the church affect your understanding of this passage. If you are a secular reader, or have a different faith commitment, think about your understanding of it. What is the identity of the suffering servant? If possible, talk to another reader who has a different perspective from you.

Most biblical scholars no longer consider christological readings of the Hebrew Bible to be appropriate, particularly in light of the anti-Semitic tradition of interpretation within the church. Reading the Hebrew Bible through the lens of Christian belief risks implying that Jewish readers do not have the full story. To avoid trivializing Jewish understandings, Christian readers of the Hebrew Bible should resist automatically looking for answers to interpretative questions in the New Testament. The books of the Hebrew Bible should be valued in their own right, as well as part of the wider canon of faith.

Our final example of a christological approach is Tim Gorringe's political liberationist reading of the Bible, which is based on the consistent call for justice throughout the Bible, particularly for the poor and oppressed. In this example, his interpretative key is Jesus' actions rather than the Christ event that typological and canonical approaches take as their starting point:

This claim would rest on the hermeneutic significance of Jesus' story for the whole biblical narrative, on Jesus' commitment to the marginalized, his teaching about service and greatness, on the fact of his crucifixion by Roman power and the way the theme of service and death is interpreted by Paul in passages such as 1 Corinthians 1–3, and Philippians 2.5ff. To read the Bible in this way is not to support just one political programme, but it does on the other hand rule out a great many. (Gorringe 1998, p. 78)

Gorringe's approach is similar to those we have already looked at that identify a core strand of teaching or critical movement within the Bible with which to interpret the whole text. He uses it to set out the limits of political interpretation of the Bible, challenging the legitimacy of political readings that do not represent a commitment to social justice and transformation.

Many Christians employ some sort of christological approach to the Bible because of their understanding of the significance of Jesus' life, death and resurrection. Using a christological lens can help Christian readers locate a text within the wider arena of their faith. However, it should be used with care and respect for the earlier meaning of the text.

Hermeneutical keys based on the readers and their context

When marginalized groups discover that dominant accounts of reality do not represent their experience, they often develop their own sources of truth. For example, in the 1980s Chuck D. of hip hop group, Public Enemy, repeatedly called rap music 'black people's CNN' (Toop 2000, p. 46) because mainstream sources of information were unable (or unwilling) to broadcast what was really happening among black communities. In response to this, hip hop artists became 'self-proclaimed contemporary prophets' offering 'truth-revealing parables and pictures' (Perry 2004, p. 2). Similarly, biblical interpreters from communities who feel their life experiences are not represented truthfully in the Bible have found other sources of knowledge with which to engage it.

We noted earlier how the Bible contains a critical dialogue between various traditions. This debate within the canon encourages contemporary readers to engage in a similar process of dialogue between the Bible and their own life experience. As we saw in Chapter 5, many committed interpretative approaches prioritize contemporary human experience over the witness of the Bible. They argue for the authority of contemporary human experience as well as the faith experience recorded in the Bible.

While most contextual interpretations encourage readers to trust insights from their lived experience, some liberation movements prioritize the insights of poor and marginalized communities over other human experience. Christian Aid's NRSV Bible (2003) illustrates this interpretative method by putting on the front cover a picture of Asebech Amha, a young Ethiopian girl. This reminds readers to approach the Bible with the needs and hopes of poor and marginalized people such as Asebech in mind. Equally, many liberationist scholars reject any biblical teaching that is experienced as harmful by marginalized peoples.

Other cultural texts and traditions

In Chapter 2 we considered how some biblical interpreters challenge the notion of a fixed canon. One such scholar, Elisabeth Schüssler Fiorenza, advocates an image of the Bible as a walled garden and encourages readers to make use of resources within and beyond the wall. She believes canonical authority should not be oppressive and restrictive but should foster 'creativity, strength and freedom' (Schüssler Fiorenza 1994, p. 11). Thus the authority of the Bible is redefined as a starting point for liberative action, encouraging the reader to explore new ideas and approaches, rather than the traditional notion of the canon functioning as a boundary marker.

Rosemary Radford Ruether also makes use of non-biblical texts in her interpretative work. One of her earliest published works, *Womanguides: Readings towards a feminist theology* (1985), was a collection of readings gathered from across the centuries (and including some biblical texts) to serve as a resource for feminist theology. Ruether did not promote this collection as a new canon but as a starting point from which such a new canon might emerge from the feminist community (Ruether 1985b, p. ix). Ruether argued that the biblical canon could not function as the only authoritative collection for women because parts of it promoted patriarchy and silence women.

Chinese scholar Kwok Pui-Lan (1995) believes Christians have to let the Christian story and their own cultural traditions inform each other (an example of the vernacular hermeneutics we looked at in Chapter 5). This involves imagination as new images are created and ancient stories reinterpreted to help the two traditions connect. She offers the example of C. S. Song's weaving together of the Chinese story of Lady Meng with the passion narrative. Such vernacular interpretations enable Christians to read the Bible alongside other local stories, affirming both as valid for faith exploration and enabling each to balance the other. Kwok suggests readers should use their 'dialogical imagination', involving active listening and openness to difference, to make real use of the resources their cultural and social context offer as they seek to discover the message of the Bible. This process gives value to different cultures and communities and suggests just as the Bible can transform culture, culture can also transform understandings of the Bible.

However, in the same collection of essays, R. S. Sugirtharajah notes two problems with using indigenous stories and symbols in dialogue with the Bible. First, the danger of idealizing traditional culture and ignoring problematic practices such as caste hierarchies. Second, he warns that the symbols and stories used may no longer be relevant or central to the grass roots communities who are struggling to survive (Sugirtharajah 1995, p. 464).

None of these scholars advocates the primacy of one text over the Bible, but most of them encourage us to look at a range of sources, of which the Bible is one among many, and see what insights emerge from the collective wisdom displayed. We should also note how using cultural texts and traditions, or collections that represent certain ideological commitments, affect the way the Bible is approached. Vernacular methods of reading may be preferred over traditional scholarly approaches. We will look at a further example of this below.

To conclude this section, we should note that most of us create our own unique interpretative lens that represents a mixture of the methods outlined above. For example, we may chose to prioritize the Gospels alongside reading with a commitment to a particular political ideology, while at the same time being influenced by interpretative methods developed through local forms of artistic expression. Finally, we should note that any interpretative lens needs to be chosen with care to ensure it does not leave us vulnerable to ideological distortion since our own cultural and social alliances often blind us to more challenging interpretations.

Reading as story

The common theme of all these interpretative approaches is that they promote dialogue within and/or beyond the Bible. Musa Dube from Botswana looks at how African women use traditional storytelling methods to reread the Bible and apply it to their own context. This method makes use of African approaches to traditions and ways of depicting life and transmitting values and wisdom. It recognizes that the story is dependent on the teller and the hearers as well as the actual story: 'The teller or writer thus does not own the story or have the last word, but rather the story is never finished: it is a page of the community's fresh and continuous reflection' (Dube 2001, p. 3).

Dube retells Mark 5.24–43, in which a woman is healed by touching Jesus on his way to heal a sick girl, as an allegory of the healing of 'Mama Africa' also suffering from years of bleeding. She concludes:

> Mama Africa is standing up. She is not talking. She is not asking. She is not offering any more money – for none is left. Mama Africa is coming up behind Jesus. She is pushing through a strong human barricade. *Weak and still bleeding but determined, she is stretching out her hand. If only she can touch the garments of Jesus Christ.* (Dube 2001, pp. 59–60, Dube's italics)

Working in Scotland, Richard Bauckham similarly suggests that rather than seeing the authority of the Bible as a set of rules, its authority should be understood as similar to that conveyed by a story. As readers, we enter into stories and are changed by them. In this, Bauckham draws on similar ground to Stanley Hauerwas. While Bauckham and Hauerwas both claim that the Bible is the most important story for Christians, Bauckham notes that the biblical story does 'hold open space' for other stories (Bauckham

1999, p. 13). Indeed, Bauckham describes the biblical story as unfinished and suggests that as readers we play a role in developing it. However, Bauckham notes that Christians believe they have been shown the conclusion of this 'great story' through the resurrection of Christ which points to the ultimate inauguration of the reign of God in heaven and earth.

For Bauckham (as with Musa Dube's storytelling method) the Bible reveals its authoritative teaching like other stories – gradually, dynamically and in a way that keeps its readers involved (Bauckham 1999, p. 18). All commands and teachings in the Bible have to be understood in the wider context of its overall narrative framework.

In common with the approach adopted in this book, Bauckham argues that the meaning of the Bible does not lie either with the text or the reader but in their interaction, as we have repeatedly observed. The otherness of the text means that readers need to pay it careful attention:

> In summary, this is a hermeneutic which requires the interpreter seriously to listen to the text and to do so as someone who listens, not in abstraction from her own context, but in deliberate awareness of her own context. It is the listening that allows the text to speak with authority and the context that allows the text to speak with relevance. (Bauckham 1999, p. 22)

Try it out

Tell (either to yourself, or to someone else) one of the following passages as a story: John 2.1–11; Esther 4.1–17. You might choose to tell them in the first person, as if you were one of the biblical characters involved. What difference does this make to your understanding of the passage? How does this method allow you to enter into the story and explore it through your own experience?

Can we read the Bible against ourselves?

Given that there are different views of the relationship between text and reader, how are we to remain open to the challenge of the Bible and ensure that our interpretative principle does not simply reinforce our existing beliefs? We should always be suspicious of readings that seem to wholly justify our actions. Likewise we should challenge readings that domesticate the Bible, making it safe. Victorian interpretations of the infancy narratives transformed the nativity into a scene of middle-class family bliss. The hymn, 'Once in Royal David's City' encourages Christian children to be 'mild, obedient, good as he'. Such domestication obscures the poverty and instability into which the evangelist suggest Jesus was born, and imports a non-biblical picture of his family life. The only biblical account of Jesus' childhood describes Jesus causing his parents great anxiety (Luke 2.41–51). And rather than mild, the child Jesus is described as strong and wise (Luke 2.40, 52).

As readers, we must be willing to be questioned by the Bible as well as questioning it. Dietrich Bonhoeffer criticized Christians in Germany who 'only read the Bible for themselves, discarding what they didn't want ... the call is also to read Scripture *over-against* ourselves, allowing Scripture to question our lives' (cited in Fowl and Jones 1991, p. 145, Bonhoeffer's italics). In a lecture entitled, 'The Church is Dead' delivered at a conference in Switzerland in 1932, Bonhoeffer asked:

> ... has it not become terrifyingly clear again and again, in everything that we have said here to one another, that we are no longer obedient to the Bible? We are more fond of our own thoughts than of the thoughts of the Bible. We no longer read the Bible seriously, we no longer read it against ourselves, but for ourselves. If the whole of our conference here is to have any great significance, it may be perhaps that of showing us that we must read the Bible in quite a different way, until we find ourselves again. (Bonhoeffer 1965, pp. 185–6)

Here is an example of how we may read the Bible against ourselves, drawing on insights from postcolonial criticism, which as we saw in Chapter 5, interprets the Bible through the lens of colonialism.

Try it out

Read Mark 5.1–20. What do you think this story is about?

For a long time western readers have been blinded to the anti-imperial teaching of Mark's Gospel because they have been conditioned to accept the Roman empire as a positive model of democracy and learning. Richard Horsley notes:

> In theological schools as well as Sunday schools we learn that in many ways, by establishing order and an elaborate network of roads, the Roman Empire made possible the spread of the Gospel by apostles such as Peter and Paul. But by and large we have little idea of the extent to which Roman imperialism created the conditions from which the mission of Jesus and the Jesus movements arose. (Horsley 2003, p. 17)

Jesus' brief yet dramatic visit across the sea of Galilee during which he heals a demoniac is often regarded as the inauguration of a mission to the Gentiles. Passages such as this offered Christian missionaries a mandate to take the gospel to the far corners of the world. But if we pay attention to Jesus' and later Mark's context, we discover that this story is not a mandate for Christian expansion and empire building. Indeed, the historical connections between Christian mission activity and western colonialism should make readers highly suspicious of any such interpretation. The social context for Jesus' mission was the Roman occupation of Palestine and the repression that accompanied it. Interpreters such as Horsley and also Ched Myers (1990) suggest Mark 5.1–20 is a coded challenge to the Roman legion stationed nearby. If then, Mark's account is read as a highly political comment on the Roman empire, what might it have to say to those readers living in the 'new empire' of today?

Bonhoeffer's warning against a cosy relationship with Scripture is still relevant. If our interpretations do not challenge us, we should investigate our assumptions more deeply to ensure we are not letting ourselves off the hook.

Can we read against the Bible?

In contrast to the previous section, some biblical interpreters believe parts of the Bible are difficult to interpret positively and therefore advocate resistance to the text, warning us to be prepared to struggle against the text when all we can see in it are perspectives or beliefs that violate us. Renita Weems argues that biblical interpretation should be a process of:

> empowering readers to judge biblical texts, to not hesitate to read against the grain of a text if needed, and to be ready to take a stand against those texts whose worldview runs counter to one's own vision of God's liberation activity in the world. (Weems 2003, p. 31)

In the search for liberative readings of the Bible, we need to distinguish between parts of the Bible that offer life and those that describe death. There are some biblical stories that serve only as a terrible record of the wrong humans can do.

A clear example of resisting the text is Phyllis Trible's approach outlined in her book *Texts of Terror* (1984), that responds to problematic texts from the Hebrew Scriptures by denouncing their moral authority. She studies stories of rape, abuse and murder and considers how these stories of abused women bear witness to ongoing patriarchal violence. By reading against these texts, Trible suggests readers can respond to the violated women of the story through a renewed commitment to justice and equality.

In Judges 11, Jephthah makes a vow to Yahweh that should he be victorious over the Ammonites, he will sacrifice 'whoever comes out of the doors to meet me' (Judg. 11.31). But in a horrific turn of events, it is his only daughter who comes dancing out to greet him on his return. Trible suggests our response should be as such:

> Like the daughters of Israel, we remember and mourn the daughter of Jephthah the Gileadite. In her death we are all diminished; by our memory she is forever hallowed. Though not a 'survivor,' she becomes an unmistakable symbol for all the courageous daughters of faithless fathers ... surely words of lament are a seemly offering, for did not the daughters of Israel mourn the daughter of Jephthah every year? (Trible 1984, p. 108)

So Trible argues that we must tell such sad stories but always against any interpretation that justifies violence. She cautions us against attempting to smooth over our discomfort by suggesting that there is any redemptive element to such innocent suffering. Rather we must employ a critical reading that 'interprets stories of outrage on behalf of their female victims in order to recover a neglected history, to remember a past that the present embodies, and to pray that these terrors shall not come to pass again' (Trible 1984, p. 3).

As interpreters, we cannot choose to ignore these difficult passages. They are part of the Bible and so it is vital that we continue to wrestle with them. Ignoring such texts leaves them open to continued misinterpretation. It is only though direct engagement with them that we can challenge the violence of such texts and their problematic interpretative history.

Paying attention to the minor characters or nameless victims that haunt the Bible is one important way to avoid repeating the violence generated by many traditional interpretations. Looking away from the violence done to small seemingly insignificant figures in a biblical story, encourages us to look away from similar acts of violence and unknown victims in our own world.

Gina Hens-Piazza offers the following strategy for reading violent texts:

1 Make use of social scientific research to ensure we understand as accurately as possible the reality of the context from which the text emerged and which it reflects. This should prevent us from making inaccurate judgements about the action of characters in the text.
2 Read stories of violence in memory of the victims within the text and beyond it.
3 Resist the promptings of the narrator or our own instincts when they lead us to justify the violence of the text or identify with the characters who are painted in the most positive light.
4 Search out counter-texts that offer alternative ways of responding to violence. (Hens-Piazza 2003, pp. 119–22)

Try it out

Read Luke 23.39–43.

Using the four-step process outlined above, explore how violence is manifest in this passage and how it might be read in a way that counters violence.

Despite the importance of attending to these difficult texts, we should not restrict our attention to them. Ken Stone notes how by focusing on texts traditionally interpreted as anti-homosexual, gay Christians have created a defensive reading of Scripture that restricts their engagement with more liberative and promising texts (Stone 2002, p. 78). Frequently, for our own well-being, we need to hear words of comfort rather than oppression. African-American writer Howard Thurman tells the following story about his grandmother:

> My regular chore was to do all of the reading for my grandmother – she could neither read nor write ... With a feeling of great temerity I asked her one day why it was that she would not let me read any of the Pauline letters. What she told me I shall never forget. 'During the days of slavery,' she said, 'the master's minister would occasionally hold services for the slaves ... Always the white minister used as his text something from Paul. At least three or four times a year he used as a text: "Slaves be obedient to them that are your masters ... as unto Christ." Then he would go on to show how, if we were good and happy slaves, God would bless us. I promised my Maker that if I ever learned to read and if freedom ever came, I would not read that part of the Bible.' (Thurman 1949, pp. 30–1)

We must seek liberation from the text: both from the potential violence of the text and by finding liberation in the text. This search for liberation is our final step in the process.

7

Our Goal – Life-Affirming Interpretations

Revisiting our start point

At the end of any process of interpretation, we need to assess how far we have come towards the goal we began with. What task, question or situation brought us to the Bible? Has our interpretative task been satisfactorily completed? In Chapter 1 we noted the importance of defining the purpose and goal of each act of biblical interpretation. At the end of the process, we assess how well our goals have been achieved.

> **Try it out**
>
> How much closer are you to understanding one of the questions you brought to the text at the start? In what ways has your question been refined by the interpretative process?

Chapter 1 noted the many different reasons for reading the Bible. The primary division could be said to be between public purposes and faith-based purposes. However, many public interpreters (including academic interpreters) work from an implicit or explicit faith perspective (or another commitment that affects their reading). Similarly, many Jewish and Christian readers, and particularly those in leadership positions, use academic scholarship to inform and enrich their reading. That said, it does matter whether the Bible is being interpreted in the context of religious faith or in an academic or other public context, because the reasons for the interpretative work and the expected outcomes are different.

For example, Litchfield (2004, p. 228) suggests that Bible study in local church groups aims to help Christians to:

- grow in discipleship;
- experience God through the Scriptures;
- grow in understanding of the Scriptures;
- seek guidance for their lives;
- form and transform themselves and their community;
- be responsible stewards of the Christian tradition;
- and develop their ethical responsibility.

Academic and public study of the Bible is carried out for a wide variety of reasons. In Chapter 3 we looked at some of the literary, historical and impact historical questions that are investigated by interpreters. In Chapter 5 we looked at the ways interpreters around the world bring the Bible into dialogue with pressing contemporary social, political, cultural, theological and ethical issues.

The public arena in which the Bible is being studied is changing. As we noted in Chapter 5, committed readings are becoming established as a valid and exciting area of academic research. Research into the impact history of the Bible is one of the most important areas of development in the field of biblical studies today. The early twenty-first century has also seen a rise in global conflicts, which some people see as foreign aggression or terrorism and others as just warfare. These conflicts are rooted, at least partly, in clashes of religious and cultural perspective. Against all the predictions of the mid-twentieth century, religion and the Bible are very much back on the agenda today. Learning to interpret the Bible is an important skill for all who wish to participate in public life. It is also a transferable skill which can help us to read the sacred texts of other religious faiths more sensitively.

Try it out

If you approach the Bible primarily from a faith perspective, think about which of the goals of academic study you also want to pursue, and visa versa. Jot these goals down for future reference.

How might you encourage dialogue across the boundaries of academy and faith communities? What opportunities do you have to read the Bible with people with different intentions or expectations from your own? Consider what insights you have gained or might gain from their readings.

Seeking healing, transformation and liberation

Whether the Bible is studied from an academic or public perspective or from a faith commitment, or a combination, the process outlined in this book suggests that all readers can share a common goal – to discover good news through dialogue with the text which can be lived out. The notion of good news may seem limited to Christian readers (after all the word 'gospel' means 'good news') but good news can take any number of forms. It can apply to a range of goals, private or communal, academic or devotional, and can alert readers to difficult truths as well as positive insights. It can offer:

- validation of the reader's experience;
- comfort or reassurance;
- healing;
- challenge – e.g. liberation for others through renouncing power or privilege;
- or denunciation of oppression (whether recorded in the Bible or perpetuated today).

The process this book sets forward argues that good news for the reader, and for others affected by their reading, is the proper goal of biblical interpretation, whether such good news accurately advances our historical understanding to help build up a clearer picture of a particular period in the formation of the Bible, or offers the reassurance of God's peace to those wanting to grow in faith.

Yet good news for some can mean bad news for others. How can interpreters adjudicate between these competing goals? One important criterion is to see whether the interpretation arrived at is good news for the poor, powerless or marginalized. This value derives from the Bible itself, which highlights God's concern for the oppressed (e.g. Exod. 3.7), aliens, widows and orphans (e.g. Deut. 24.17) repeatedly. By giving priority to the questions and needs of the most vulnerable, interpreters can be confident that readings are truly life-affirming for all. Thus the aim of biblical interpretation should be to engage in conversation between text and context to find, and realize, good news that nurtures life for all, but especially those who need help the most.

Because much of the Bible is about people's encounters with a God who is presented as good and as caring for the whole natural order, there are many, many passages in it that offer good news to readers. Most theological readings of the Bible begin with the principle that God is good, that God's world is good, and that God's purposes for all of it are good. Such readings also recognize that this is not always evident in human experience. Indeed, people sometimes experience God and the world as sources of suffering and evil instead. Also, as we have seen, human liberation can sometimes be hard to find among difficult passages and in the face of legacies of damaging interpretation. The figure of Jacob wrestling with the angel until the break of day (Gen. 32.22–32) can serve as a model for biblical interpreters who also must sometimes struggle to extract blessing from the Bible.

Filipina theologian, Muriel Orevillo-Montenegro recalls how following her rejection of a god who inflicted suffering, she 'searched diligently' for the true God of love (Orevillo-Montenegro 2000, p. 59). Her experience of communal struggle encouraged her to look for a liberating word for the oppressed within the biblical narrative. In a similar way, William Abraham's notion of the canon as a space for formation leads him to see how, 'Scripture functions to bring one to faith, to make one wise unto salvation, to force one to wrestle with awkward questions about violence and the poor, to comfort those in sorrow, and to nourish hope for the redemption of the world' (Abraham 1998, pp. 6–7).

Some interpreters argue that the Bible itself advocates methods of reading that promote peace, justice and love. We saw in Chapter 3 that Ulrich Luz suggests using Jesus' radical love as 'a criterion of truth' for biblical interpretation and application (Luz 1994, p. 96). This should lead readers to reject interpretations that do not promote more loving ways of living in the world. Néstor Míguez brings together the criterion of love and justice, recognizing that biblical interpretation has an impact beyond the reader. He argues, 'interpretation is not only an intellectual exercise; it is also a liberating experience of overcoming injustice, a living experience of loving others' (Míguez 2004, p. 10).

Although it has at times failed to do so, the institutional church is committed to reading and enacting the Bible in ways that enable the flourishing of life. This has led individual church leaders and public gatherings of leaders such as church synods to challenge interpretations of the Bible that cause social harm. The Vatican warns against, 'every attempt at actualization set in a direction contrary to evangelical justice and charity, such as, for example, the use of the Bible to justify racial segregation, anti-semitism or sexism' (The Pontifical Biblical Commission 1993, cited in Houlden 1995, p. 85).

Try it out

Obtain a copy of a weekly church newspaper, or tune in to programmes like the BBC's *Thought for the Day* on Radio 4, to identify how religious leaders seek to offer socially constructive interpretations of the Bible in relation to a current issue.

Do you support their views?

Chapter 1 proposed that we should aim to provide provisional yet responsible interpretations of the Bible. Provisional readings acknowledge that though our context as readers is always changing, we can still offer interpretations of the Bible for the here and now. Being a responsible interpreter requires us to work with integrity, paying close attention to ourselves and to the text before us. This requires us to be both consistent and dynamic in our interaction with the Bible.

Be consistent

To be consistent in our handling of the text, we should always come to the text from where we are and with an awareness of the wider situation from which we read. As Chapter 2 reminds us, we need to be aware of how we view the Bible and why we see it in this way. We should also be attentive to the actual text and diligent in our attempts to understand it. As we noted in Chapter 3, there are a range of exegetical tools at our disposal. As responsible interpreters we should always try to use the tools best suited to the task and passage we are working on, and be willing to try out new methods where necessary. If we have a commitment to reading as part of a particular community (the church, a social or ethnic group, as a New Testament scholar, etc.) we must also be upfront about that and how it informs our reading. Furthermore, responsible interpretation takes account of the work done by other readers, both in the academy and at a popular and devotional level.

Being consistent should prevent us from letting the text or ourselves off the hook by applying a different interpretative strategy to difficult or challenging texts. It requires us to remain open to the text and to ourselves and to recognize when our dialogue provokes new definitions of ourselves, the world or our beliefs.

Be dynamic

Seeking out life-affirming interpretations should also encourage us to be dynamic in our relationship with the Bible. The open-ended and dialogical nature of the text encourages us to go beyond surface readings, noting divergence and movement, and keeping the text open to a range of meanings.

Moreover, as we noted in the previous chapter, from a Christian perspective the Bible is perceived as telling an unfinished story which will only be completed with the coming of God's kingdom. This openness suggests the reader has a role in shaping the ongoing story of the Bible's interaction with the world. Richard Bauckham notes:

> The *unfinished* nature of the biblical story – or, more positively, the eschatological hope as the ultimate future God will give to his world – is what

creates the space for finding ourselves and our contemporary world in the biblical story. It is what enables and requires the hermeneutic of listening in context that we have briefly suggested. It is what resists the premature closure that would stifle the freedom of obedient Christian living in the contemporary world. (Bauckham 1999, p. 23 his italics)

Such an understanding of the process of reading gives the reader responsibility for developing the story. The World Council of Churches notes the responsibility of the church to anticipate the coming kingdom of justice and peace in its response to the Bible:

Just as Scripture constantly looks forward in hope to God's future, the interpreting activity of the Church is also an anticipatory projection of the reality of the reign of God, which is both already present and yet to come. Reading 'the signs of the times,' both in the history of the past and in the events of the present, is to be done in the context of the announcement of 'the new things to come'; this orientation to the future is part of the reality of the Church as an hermeneutical community. Therefore the struggle for peace, justice and the integrity of creation, the renewed sense of mission in witness and service, the liturgy in which the Church proclaims and celebrates the promise of God's reign and its coming in the praxis of faith, are all integral parts of the constant interpretative task of the Church. (World Council of Churches 1998, pp. 19–20)

In Chapter 4 we explored the nature of our identity as readers. These are both specific to any one moment and context, and changing as we move through life, having new experiences, moving to new places and taking up new roles. Awareness of our changing life situation and attitude towards the Bible should stop us being overconfident that we hold the definitive interpretation of any text. What we need is a working interpretation that equips us for action. We can later reassess our earlier readings and modify them based on the experience of testing them out in practice. This process of action and reflection is known as the hermeneutical circle, as shown in the diagram on page 188.

The idea of a dynamic circle that keeps open the conversation between our context and the text was developed by the philosopher Martin Heidegger

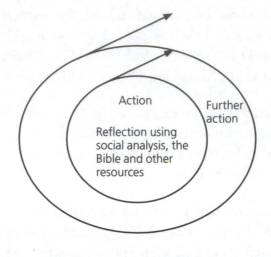

The Hermeneutical Circle

(1889–1976), though the theologian Friedrich Schleiermacher (1768–1834) had already noted that words, texts and contexts interact in a mutually revising way (Soulen and Soulen 2001, p. 73). Rudolf Bultmann in turn pointed out that the quality of the life questions put to the text at the start of the process determine the quality of the answers the hermeneutical circle produces, because prior understanding is needed to hear a text well (Bultmann 1950, p. 90).

In more recent times the hermeneutical circle has been widely adopted by liberation theologians, particularly those working in Latin America. These theologians begin all interpretation from their lived experience. Practical action is the first stage and precedes reflection on the Bible and the situation of the interpreter. With action as the driving force, this approach forces readers to keep open the dialogue between text and context. Reflection can lead to action, but by starting with action we are provoked to more specific and rigorous reflection on what we are doing because we know we shall be using the result of our reflection to guide the next stage of our action. Thus, action helps to ground and focus our reflection on and interpretation of the Bible. Juan Luis Segundo argues, 'each new reality obliges us to interpret the word of God afresh, to change reality accordingly, and then to go back and reinterpret the word of God again, and so on' (Segundo 1976, p. 8).

The hermeneutical circle is actually more of a spiral, which develops deeper understandings of the text and context with each rotation. It shows why we can never complete our study of a biblical passage. We come to the text each time at a different stage in our life, bothered with particular concerns, and so always approach it from a unique place. So, although the text itself remains fixed, our response to it is different each time.

Try it out

One of the authors spent an academic term studying the story of Cain and Abel (Gen. 4.1–16) and with each reading discovered something new. As the term progressed, the events of the world, the church calendar, and her own changing circumstances all created new questions to approach the text with.

Why not choose one Bible passage to live with for a few months, to see how your changing life affects your interaction with it?

Biblical texts do not only repay rereading in this way because of the changing circumstances of our lives, but also because of the long processes involved in their formation and their reception. Each passage echoes the voices and perspectives which affected its development and resonates with other stories within and beyond the biblical canon.

Reading the same text repeatedly helps us distinguish between what remains the same and what changes. The words in the text remain the same, though even these have been subject to some change during the development and transmission of the text. Our own perspectives and judgements, and the culture we live in, are all subject to change. As we listen to the text and engage with the world in positive ways, we know that our interpretations of the text may change in the future.

Brian Blount points out that change is a consequence of being alive and attentive:

> since we're always changing, and our contexts are always changing, the words that interpret the whisper of God's Spirit in our time must

necessarily be changing as well. God, you remember Jesus saying, is a God of the living, not of the dead. But a last word is necessarily a dead word. It stops listening. It stops learning. It stops living! ... *Nothing that is living is ever last*. A living word is always a beginning word. (Blount 2002, pp. 56–7, Blount's italics)

To take another image – we trace our provisional readings of the Bible in the swirling dance between text and context. Through disciplined yet lively activity, we explore what we and those who are still strangers to us, need to know here and now. This accords well with the Christian understanding of God's activity as a loving dance of creation, restoration and constant renewal.

Try it out

Helder Camera encouraged readers of the Bible to, 'Honor the word eternal/ And speak to make a new world possible' (Camera cited in Morley 1992, p. 158).

Read 1 Thessalonians 5.12–28. How might your interpretation of this passage open up new possibilities and ways of acting well in the world, while honouring the 'word eternal'?

In his book, *Defenseless Flower*, Carlos Mesters notes of poor communities in Latin America:

The people's main interest is not to interpret the Bible, but to interpret life with the help of the Bible. They try to be faithful, not primarily to the meaning the text has in itself (the historical and literal meaning), but to the meaning they discover in the text for their own lives ... The Bible of life was their lives, in which they tried to put into practice and incarnate the word of God. And it was even more: life itself is for them the place where God speaks. (Mesters 1989, p. 9)

The ultimate purpose of biblical interpretation is not understanding, but healing, transformation and liberation. It is to enable people to live and flourish. Therefore we end as we began, committed to an ongoing quest for life-affirming interpretations of the Bible, open to the faith perspectives of these ancient texts, even if we do not share these ourselves. The Bible is about human encounters with God. When we interpret the Bible we participate in the ongoing exploration of the many different ways in which God's liberating and transforming love is revealed to humanity.

Summary of the Interpretative Process

1 Where do we want to go?

This step in the interpretative process asks you to:
- identify your overall reason for studying the Bible;
- identify your interpretative focus in studying a particular passage, and understand how that focus affects your reading of the passage;
- be clear about the questions you begin with, even if these are different from the ones you end up with;
- work towards a provisional and responsible interpretation of a passage.

2 Past experience and present expectations

This step in the interpretative process asks you to:
- take account of the Bible's status and influence in your own and other contexts;
- recognize the impact of the Bible on social structures;
- make responsible use of a range of cultural interpretations of the Bible;
- take account of the unfamiliar nature of the Bible, both as an ancient near eastern text and as a text that is regarded by some as divine;
- identify your own understanding of the Bible's authority;

- read the Bible as a whole, and make use of intertextual methods of interpretation;
- identify your own extended canon and make appropriate use of it;
- recognize the value of central and marginal texts;
- note how the use of a lectionary shapes a faith community's interaction with the Bible;
- consider how you resolve tensions and differences within the Bible.

3 Tools for exegesis

This step in the interpretative process asks you to:
- become familiar with a text through a range of methods including copying out and memorizing;
- use discourse analysis to analyse the structure and composition of a text in detail;
- use narrative criticism to identify and explore narrative features such as events, characters and narrative strategies;
- read a text in the original language or make use of a range of translations;
- make use of the insights of textual criticism;
- recognize how words develop over time and the need to explore the historical meaning of a word or phrase in a text;
- use form criticism to identify earlier oral use of a text and its genre;
- use source criticism to identify earlier written sources of a multiple source text;
- use tradition criticism to locate the text within wider cycles of narrative and traditions;
- use redaction criticism to consider the theological beliefs of the final author or editor of a text;
- make use of information concerning the wider social, political and religious background of a text;
- use impact history methods to explore how a text has been received and its influence over time.

4 Our reality

This step in the interpretative process asks you to:
• recognize the role of the reader in creating the meaning of a text;
• describe your own identity and begin to consider how different aspects affect your interpretation, including: gender and sexuality; ethnicity; age, ability and well-being; socio-economic status and political affiliation; denominational, spiritual and theological traditions;
• undertake social analysis of your context, through careful observation and the use of an appropriate method of analysis;
• consider the communities to which you belong and how you read the Bible as part of them.

5 Committed readings

This step in the interpretative process asks you to:
• recognize how your commitments affect your reading;
• take account of readings from different parts of the world, including post-colonial critical readings and vernacular readings;
• identify your own ideological commitments, those of the text and those of other methods, including feminist criticism, social scientific criticism, and deconstruction and postmodern approaches;
• recognize how reading from a faith perspective influences interpretation, including noting the affect of spiritual reading methods, hearing the Bible in a context of worship, canonical critical methods, and readings that nurture discipleship;
• make good use of commentaries.

6 Enabling dialogue with the text

This step in the interpretative process asks you to:
• see interpretation as a form of dialogue;

- consider how the context of a text and the context of interpretation relate to each other;
- identify your hermeneutical key(s) from the Bible, a faith perspective or your own experience and context;
- practise reading the Bible as story and note how this opens up space for dialogue between a text and your context;
- allow space for the Bible to critique your interpretation;
- resist violent or other harmful interpretations of the Bible.

7 Our goal – life-affirming interpretations

This step in the interpretative process asks you to:
- revisit your starting point in the interpretative process;
- consider the different academic and faith-based reasons for studying the Bible and how there can be dialogue between them;
- be consistent and yet dynamic in your interpretation;
- commit to life-affirming interpretations of the Bible.

References and Further Reading

Abraham, W. J. (1998) *Canon and Criterion in Christian Theology*, Oxford: Oxford University Press.

Aharoni, Y. and Hav-Yonah, M. (1968) *The Macmillan Bible Atlas*, New York and London: Macmillan.

Allen, R. J. (1987) *Contemporary Biblical Interpretation for Preaching*, Valley Forge: Judson Press.

Augustine (397, 426) *On Christian Doctrine*, R. P. H. Green (ed.), (1995) Oxford: Oxford University Press.

Aune, D. (1997–8) *Revelation*, 3 vols, Word Biblical Commentary, Dallas: Word.

Bailey, R. C. (1998) 'The Danger of Ignoring One's Own Cultural Bias in Interpreting the Text' in R. S. Sugirtharajah (ed.), *The Postcolonial Bible*, Sheffield: Sheffield Academic Press, pp. 66–90.

Barton, J. (ed.) (1998) *The Cambridge Companion to Biblical Interpretation*, Cambridge: Cambridge University Press.

Barton, J. (2002) *The Biblical World*, 2 vols, London: Routledge.

Barton, S. C. (1995), 'Historical Criticism and Social Scientific Perspectives in New Testament Study' in J. B. Green (ed.), *Hearing the New Testament: Strategies for interpretation*, Grand Rapids and Carlisle: Eerdmans and Paternoster, pp. 61–89.

Bauckham, R. (1983) *Jude, 2 Peter*, Word Biblical Commentary 50, Waco: Word Books.

Bauckham, R. (1999) *Scripture and Authority Today*, Cambridge: Grove.

Bauer, D. R. (2003) *An Annotated Guide to Biblical Resources for Ministry*, Peabody, MA: Hendrickson.

Beckford, R. (2001) *God of the Rahtid: Redeeming rage,* London: Darton, Longman and Todd.

Berger, K. (1999) 'Form Criticism, New Testament' in J. H. Hayes (ed.), *Dictionary of Biblical Interpretation*, vol. 1, Nashville: Abingdon.

Berlin, A. and Brettler, M. Z. (2004) *The Jewish Study Bible*, Oxford: Oxford University Press.

Birch, B. C. and Rasmussen, L. L. (1989) *Bible and Ethics in the Christian Life*, Minneapolis: Augsburg.

Block, J. W. (2002) *Copious Hosting: A theology of access for people with disabilities*, New York: Continuum.

Blount, B. K. (2002) 'The Last Word in Biblical Authority', in W. Brueggemann, W. C. Placher and B. K. Blount, *Struggling with Scripture*, Louisville: Westminister John Knox Press, pp. 51–69.

Bockmuehl, M. (1998) 'To Be or Not to Be: The possible futures of New Testament scholarship', *Scottish Journal of Theology*, 51(3): 271–306.

Boff, C. (1987) *Theology and Praxis: Epistemological foundations*, Maryknoll, NY: Orbis.

Bonhoeffer, D. (1965) *No Rusty Swords: Letters, lectures and notes 1928–1936 from the collected works of Dietrich Bonhoeffer Vol. 1* (trans. Edwin H. Robertson and John Bowden, ed. Edwin H. Robertson), London: Collins.

Brotzman, E. R. (1994) *Old Testament Textual Criticism: A practical introduction*, Grand Rapids: Baker.

Brueggemann, W. (1997a) *Cadences of Home: Preaching among exiles*, Louisville, KT: Westminster John Knox Press.

Brueggemann, W. (1997b) *Theology of the Old Testament: Testimony, advocacy*, Minneapolis: Fortress Press.

Brueggemann, W., Placher, W. C. and Blount, B. K. (2002) *Struggling with Scripture*, Louisville: Westminister John Knox Press.

Bultmann, R. (1950) 'The Problem of Hermeneutics' in *New Testament and Mythology and Other Basic Writings*, ed. and trans. S. M. Ogden (1984), Philadelphia: Fortress Press, pp. 69–93.

Callaway, M. C. (1999) 'Canonical Criticism' in S. L. McKenzie and S. R. Haynes (eds) *To Each Its Own Meaning: An introduction to biblical criticisms and their application*, revised and expanded third edition, Louisville: Westminster John Knox Press, pp. 142–55.

Cannon, K. (1995), *Katie's Canon*, New York: Continuum.

Cardenal, E. (1982) *The Gospel in Solentiname, Volume IV*, D. D. Walsh (trans.), Maryknoll, NY: Orbis.

Carson, D. A. (1993) *New Testament Commentary Survey*, fourth ed., Leicester: IVP.

Cave, N. (1998) *Introduction to Mark*, Edinburgh: Canongate Books.

Childs, B. (1979) *Introduction to the Old Testament as Scripture*, Philadelphia: Fortress.

Childs, B. (1985a) *Old Testament Theology in a Canonical Context*, Philadelphia: Fortress.

Childs, B. (1985b) *The New Testament as Canon: An introduction*, Philadelphia: Fortress.

Christian Aid (2004) *Trade Justice*, London: Church House Publishing.

CMS/USPG/The Methodist Church (2004) *The Christ We Share*, CMS/USPG/The Methodist Church.

Coggins, R. J. and Houlden, J. L. (eds) (1990) *A Dictionary of Biblical Interpretation*, London: SCM Press.

Dawes, S. (2004) 'Revelation in Methodism' in C. Marsh et al. (eds) *Unmasking Methodist Theology*, London: Continuum, pp. 109–17.

De Silva, D. A. (2004) *An Introduction to the New Testament: Contexts, methods and ministry formation*, Downer's Grove, Illinois and Leicester: InterVarsity Press and Apollos.

Dietrich, W. and Luz, U. (2002) *The Bible in a World Context: An experiment in cultural hermeneutics*, Grand Rapids and Cambridge: Eerdmans.

Divarkar SJ, P. (ed.) and Malatesta SJ, E. J. (1991) *Ignatius of Loyola: Spiritual exercises and selected works (The Classics of Western Spirituality'series)* Mahwah NJ: Paulist Press.

Dube, M. W. (ed.) (2001) *Other Ways of Reading: African women and the Bible*, Atlanta: SBL/ Geneva: WCC.

Dube, M. W. (2003) 'Jumping the Fire with Judith: Postcolonial feminist hermeneutics of liberation' in Silvia Schroer and Sophia Bietenhard (eds) *Feminist Interpretation of the Bible and the Hermeneutic of Liberation*, London: Sheffield Academic Press, pp. 60–76.

Dyer, Richard (1997) *White*, London: Routledge.

Elliger, K. and Rudolph, W. (eds) (1977) *Biblia Hebraica Stuttgartensia*, second edition, edited by W. Rudolph and H. P. Rüger, Stuttgart: Deutsche Bibelgesellschaft.

Elliot, J. K. (2000) 'Christian Apocrypha' in Adrian Hastings, Alistair Mason and Hugh Pyper (eds) *The Oxford Companion to Christian Thought*, Oxford: Oxford University Press, pp. 30–1.

Erbele-Kuster, D. (2004) 'Rereading the Bible: A dialogue with women theologians from Latin America, Africa and Asia' in *Voices from the Third World*, Vol. XXVII(1) June 2004, pp. 53–67.

Fabella, V. and Sugirtharajah, R. S. (eds) (2000) *Dictionary of Third World Theologies*, Maryknoll, NY: Orbis.

Farmer, K., (1998) 'Psalms 42–89' in Farmer, W. R., et al. (eds) *The International Bible Commentary: A catholic and ecumenical commentary for the twenty-first century*, Collegeville: The Liturgical Press.

Farmer, W. R., McEvenue, S., Levoratti, Armando J. and Dungan, D. L., (eds) (1998) *The International Bible Commentary: A catholic and ecumenical commentary for the twenty-first century*, Collegeville: The Liturgical Press.

Ferguson, E. (2003) *Backgrounds of Early Christianity*, third revised edition, Grand Rapids: Eerdmans.

Fowl, S. E., and Jones, L. G. (1991) *Reading in Communion: Scripture and ethics in Christian life*, London: SPCK.

Fowler, R. M., Blumhofer, E., and Segovia, F. F. (eds) (2004) *New Paradigms for Bible Study: The Bible in the third millennium*, New York: T and T Clark.

Freire, P. [1973] (1993) *Pedagogy of the Oppressed*, London: Penguin.

Gillingham, S. E. (1998) *One Bible Many Voices: Different approaches to biblical studies*, London: SPCK.

Gnuse, R. (1985) *The Authority of the Bible: Theories of inspiration, revelation and the canon of scripture*, Mahwah, NJ: Paulist Press.

Gnuse, Robert, (1999) 'Tradition History' in Hayes, J. H. (ed.) *Dictionary of Biblical Interpretation*, vol. 2, Nashville: Abingdon.

Gorman, M. (2001) *Elements of Biblical Exegesis: A basic guide for students and ministers*, Peabody, MA: Hendrikson.

Gorringe, T. (1998) 'Political readings of Scripture' in Barton, J. (ed.) *The Cambridge Companion to Biblical Interpretation*, Cambridge: Cambridge University Press, pp. 67–80.

Goss, R. E. and West, M. (eds) (2000) *Take Back the Word: A queer reading of the Bible*, Cleveland, OH: The Pilgrim Press.

Graham, H. (1999), 'Matthew 5:1–12: An Asian perspective' in *Return to Babel: Global perspectives on the Bible*, J. R. Levison and Pope-Levison, P. (eds), Louisville, Kentucky: Westminster John Knox.

Green, D. and Melamed, C. (2000) *A Human Development Approach to Globalisation*, London: Christian Aid/ CAFOD.

Grieb, A. K. (2002) 'Deutero-Pauline Letters' in W. Howard-Brook and S. Ringe (eds) *The New Testament: Introducing the way of discipleship*, Maryknoll NY: Orbis, pp. 148–67.

Gunn, David M. (1999) 'Narrative Criticism' in S. L. McKenzie and S. R. Haynes (eds) *To Each Its Own Meaning: An introduction to biblical criticisms and their application*, revised and expanded third edition, Louisville: Westminster John Knox Press, pp. 201–29.

Gutiérrez, G. (1988) *A Theology of Liberation: History, politics and salvation*, Maryknoll: Orbis.

Hammer, R. (trans., intro., and comm.) and Goldin, J. (preface) (1995) *The Classic Midrash, Tannaitic Commentaries on the Bible* ('The Classics of Western Spirituality' series) Mahwah NJ: Paulist Press.

Haney, E. H. (1998) *The Great Commandment,* Cleveland OH: The Pilgrim Press.

Hauerwas, S. (1983) *The Peaceable Kingdom*, Notre Dame, IN: University of Notre Dame.

Hayes, J. H. (ed.) (1999) *Dictionary of Biblical Interpretation*, 2 vols, Nashville: Abingdon.

Hens-Piazza, G. (2003) *Nameless, Blameless and Without Shame: Two cannibal mothers before a king,* Collegeville, MN: Liturgical Press.

Hill, L. (1998), 'Final Hour' in *The Miseducation of Lauryn Hill*, Philadelphia: Ruff-House Records.

Holgate, D. A. (1993) 'Making the Text Our Own', *Expository Times* 104 (8): 232–6.

Holland, J. and Henriot SJ, P. (1983) *Social Analysis Linking Faith and Justice*, Maryknoll NY: Orbis.

Holloway, R. (2002) *Doubts and Love: What is left of Christianity* Edinburgh: Canongate.

Houlden, J. L. (ed.) (1995) *The Interpretation of the Bible in the Church*, London: SCM Press, containing The Pontifical Biblical Commission (1993) *The Interpretation of the Bible in the Church*, The Vatican: Libreria Editrice Vaticana.

Horsley, R. A. (2002) *Jesus and Empire: The kingdom of God and the new world disorder,* Minneapolis: Augsburg.

Howard-Brook W. and Ringe, S. (eds) (2002) *The New Testament: Introducing the way of discipleship*, Maryknoll NY: Orbis.

Hull, J. (2001) *In the Beginning There Was Darkness: A blind person's conversations with the Bible*, London: SCM Press.

Jansson, T. (2003) *The Summer Book*, London: Sort of Books.

Joy, C. I. D. (2001) *Revelation: A post-colonial viewpoint*, Delhi: Indian Society for Promoting Christian Knowledge.

Kahl, B. 'Fratricide and Ecocide: Re-reading Gen. 2–4' in *Earth Habitat: Eco-justice and the church's response*, ed. D. Hessel and L. Rasmussen, Minneapolis: Fortress Press, 2001, pp. 53–68.

Katusno-Ishii, L. and Orteza, E. J. (eds) (2000), *Of Rolling Waters and Roaring Wind,* Geneva: World Council of Churches.

Kovacs, J., Rowland, C. and Callow, R. (2004) *Revelation*, Blackwell Bible Commentaries, Oxford: Blackwells.

Kwok, Pui-lan (1995) 'Discovering the Bible in the Non-Biblical World' in R. S. Sugirtharajah, R. S. *Voices from the Margins: Interpreting the Bible in the third world*, London: SPCK, pp. 289–306.

Kwok, P. l. (2005) *Postcolonial Imagination and Feminist Theology*, London: SCM-Canterbury Press.

Levison, J. R. and Pope-Levison, P. (eds) (1999) *Return to Babel: Global perspectives on the Bible,* Louisville KY: Westminster John Knox.

Litchfield, R. G. (2004) 'Rethinking Local Bible Study in a Postmodern Era' in R. M. Fowler, E. Blumhofer and F. F. Segovia (eds) (2004) *New Paradigms for Bible Study: The Bible in the third millennium,* New York: T and T Clark.

Longman III, T. (2003) *Old Testament Commentary Survey,* third edition, Leicester: Inter-Varsity Press.

Luz, U. (1989) *Matthew 1–7: A commentary,* trans. W. C. Linss, Edinburgh: T and T Clark.

Luz, U. (1994) *Matthew in History: Interpretation, influence and effects,* Minneapolis: Fortress Press.

Luz, U. (2001) *Matthew 8–20,* trans. J. E. Crouch, Hermeneia, Minneapolis: Fortress Press.

MacDonald, M. Y. (1988) *The Pauline Churches,* SNTSMS 60, Cambridge: Cambridge University Press.

Maduro, O. (2000) 'Social Analysis' in V. Fabella, M. M. and R. S. Sugirtharajah (eds) *Dictionary of Third World Theologies* Maryknoll NY: Orbis, pp. 185–7.

Malherbe, A. J. (1987) *Paul and the Thessalonians,* Philadelphia: Fortress Press.

Malherbe, A. J. (2000) *The Letters to the Thessalonians,* Anchor Bible Vol. 32B, New York: Doubleday.

Marx, S. (2000) *Shakespeare and the Bible,* Oxford: Oxford University Press

McKenzie S. L. and S. R. Haynes (eds) (1999) *To Each Its Own Meaning: An introduction to biblical criticisms and their application,* revised and expanded third edition, Louisville: Westminster John Knox.

Mead, J. (2002) *A Telling Place,* Glasgow: Wild Goose Publications.

Mesters, C. (1989) *Defenseless Flower: A new reading of the Bible,* Maryknoll NY: Orbis.

Metzger, B. (1994) *A Textual Commentary on the Greek New Testament,* second edition, Stuttgart: United Bible Societies.

Míguez, N. O. (2004) 'Latin American Reading of the Bible. Experiences, Challenges and its Practice' in *Journal of Latin American Hermeneutics,* 2004/1, Instituto Universitario ISEDET online version.

Moore, S. (2001) *God's Beauty Parlor and Other Queer Spaces in and Around the Bible,* Palo Alto, CA: Stanford University Press.

Morley, J. (1992) *Bread of Tomorrow,* London: SPCK.

Muddiman, John, (1990) 'Form Criticism' in Coggins, R. J. and Houlden, J. L. (eds) (1990) *A Dictionary of Biblical Interpretation,* London: SCM Press, pp. 240–3.

Myers, C. (1990) *Binding the Strong Man: Political reading of Mark's story of Jesus,* Maryknoll NY: Orbis.

Nestle, E. and K., Aland, B., Karavidopoulos, J., Martini, C. M. and Metzger, B. M. (eds) (1993) *Novum Testamentum Graece*, twenty-seventh edition, Stuttgart: Deutsche Bibelgesellschaft.

Nestle, E. and K. and Aland, B. et al. (eds) (1998) *The Greek New Testament*, fourth edition, New York: United Bible Societies.

Newsom, C. and Ringe, S. H. (eds) (1998) *Women's Bible Commentary*, expanded edition, Louisville: Westminster John Knox.

Norris, K. (1998) *Amazing Grace: A Vocabulary of faith*, Oxford: Lion.

Norris, K. (1996) *Cloister Walk*, Oxford: Lion.

Norris, K. (1993) *Dakota: A Spiritual Geography*, Boston MA: Houghton Mifflin (Trade).

Nouwen, H. J. M. (1994) *The Return of the Prodigal Son: A story of homecoming*, London: Darton, Longman and Todd.

O'Donnell OP, G. (1990) 'Reading for Holiness: Lectio Divina' in R. Maas, R. and G. O'Donnell OP (1990) *Spiritual Traditions for the Contemporary Church*, Nashville: Abingdon Press, pp. 45–54.

Oduyoye, M. A. (1990) 'The Empowering Spirit' in S. B. Thisethwaite and M. P. Engel (eds) *Lift Every Voice: Constructing Christian theologies from the underside*, San Francisco: Harper and Row, pp. 245–58.

Økland, J. (2002) 'The Excluded Gospels and their Readers, or: How to Tell when a Kiss is just a Kiss' in *The Many Voices of the Bible*, Concilium 2002/1, London: SCM Press, pp. 68–76.

Orevillo-Montenegro, M. (2000) 'Why Are Some People Cast So Low? – Feminist Theology and the Problem of Evil', *Voices from the Third World* 23(1): 51–77.

Paterson, G. (2001) *AIDS and the African Churches: Exploring the challenges*, London: Christian Aid.

Patte, D. et al. (eds) (2004) *Global Bible Commentary*, Nashville: Abingdon Press.

Pereira, N. C. (2003) 'Changing Season: About the Bible and Other Sacred Texts in Latin America', in S. Schroer and S. Bietenhard (eds) *Feminist Interpretation of the Bible and the Hermeneutic of Liberation*, London: Sheffield Academic Press, pp. 48–58.

Perry, I. (2004) *Prophets of the Hood: Politics and poetics in hip hop*, Durham and London: Duke University Press.

Pervo, R. I. (1987) *Profit with Delight: The literary genre of the Acts of the Apostles*, Philadelphia: Fortress Press.

Placher, W. C. (2002) 'Struggling with Scripture' in W. Brueggemann, W. C. Placher, and B. K. Blount, *Struggling with Scripture*, Louisville: Westminister John Knox Press, pp. 32–50.

Porter, J. R. (2001) *The Lost Bible*, London: Duncan Baird Publishers.

Powell, M. A. (1999) 'Narrative Criticism' in J. B. Green (ed.), *Hearing the New Testament: Strategies for Interpretation*, Grand Rapids and Carlisle: Eerdmans and Paternoster, pp. 239–55.

Pressler, C. (1996) 'Biblical Criticism' in L. M. Russell and J. Shannon Clarkson (eds) *Dictionary of Feminist Theologies*, London: Mowbray.

Pressler, C. (1998) 'To Heal and Transform: Women's Biblical Studies' in Farmer, W. R., et al. (eds) *The International Bible Commentary: A catholic and ecumenical commentary for the twenty-first century*, Collegeville: The Liturgical Press.

Prior, M. CM (1997) *The Bible and Colonialism: A moral critique*, Sheffield: Sheffield Academic Press.

Pyper, H. (2000) 'Jewish Apocrypha' in Adrian Hastings, Alistair Mason and Hugh Pyper (eds) *The Oxford Companion to Christian Thought*, Oxford: Oxford University Press, p. 31.

Reardon, B. P. (1989) *Collected Ancient Greek Novels*, Berkeley: University of California Press.

Rhoads, D., Dewey, J. and Michie, D. (1999) *Mark as Story: An introduction to the narrative of a gospel*, second edition, Minneapolis: Fortress.

Rhoads, D. (ed.) (2005) *From Every People and Nation: The book of revelation in intercultural perspective*, Minneapolis: Fortress Press.

Richard, P. (1990) '1492: The Violence of God and the Future of Christianity' in Boff, L. and Elizondo, V. (eds) *1492–1992: The Voice of the Victims*, Concilium 1990/6, London: SCM Press, pp. 56–67.

Riches, J. (2004) 'Ephesians' in Patte, D. et al. (eds) *Global Bible Commentary*, Nashville: Abingdon Press.

Ringe, S. (1998) 'When Women Interpret the Bible' in Newsom, C. and Ringe, S. H. (eds), *Women's Bible Commentary*, expanded edition, Louisville: Westminster John Knox.

Rogerson, J. W. and Davies, P. (2005), *The Old Testament World*, second revised and expanded edition, London and New York: Continuum.

Radford Ruether, R. (1983) *Sexism and God-talk*, London: SCM Press.

Radford Ruether, R. (1985) 'Feminist Interpretation: A Method of Correlation' in Letty M. Russell (ed.) *Feminist Interpretations of the Bible*, New York: Blackwell, pp. 111–24.

Radford Ruether, R. (1985b) *Womanguides Readings Towards a Feminist Theology* Boston: Beacon Press.

Rogerson, J. and Davies, P. (2005) *The Old Testament World*, third revised and expanded edition, London: T & T Clark.

Rowland, C. (1998) 'The Book of Revelation' in *New Interpreters Bible* xii, Nashville: Abingdon.

Rowland, C. (2005) 'Imaging the Apocalypse' *New Testament Studies* 51 (3): 303–27.

Rowland, C. and Corner, M. (1990) *Liberating Exegesis: The challenge of liberation theology to biblical studies*, London: SPCK.

Schell, E. L. (1998) *Quilting Anthology: Scraps*, New York: unpublished.

Schneiders, Sandra (1997) Interpreting the Bible: The right and the responsibility, Scripture from Scratch published online at www.americancatholic.org/Newsletters/SFS/an0997.asp accessed 14 May 2004.

Schroer, S. (2003) 'We Will Know Each Other by Our Fruits', in S. Schroer and S. Bietenhard (eds) *Feminist Interpretation of the Bible and the Hermeneutic of Liberation*, London: Sheffield Academic Press, pp. 1–16.

Schüssler Fiorenza, E. (1983) *In Memory of Her: A Feminist Theological Reconstruction of Christian Origins*, New York: Crossroad.

Schüssler Fiorenza, E. (1984a) 'Emerging Issues in Feminist Biblical Interpretation' in J. L. Weidmam (ed.) (1984) *Christian Feminism: Visions of a new humanity*, San Francisco: Harper and Row.

Schüssler Fiorenza, E. (1984b), 'Women-Church: The Hermeneutical Center of Feminist Biblical Interpretation' in *Bread Not Stone: The Challenge of Feminist Biblical Interpretation*, edited by E. Schüssler Fiorenza, Boston: Beacon Press, pp. 1–22.

Schüssler Fiorenza, E. (1994) 'Introduction: Transgressing Canonical Boundaries' in E. Schüssler Fiorenza ed. *Searching the Scriptures vol ii: A feminist commentary*, New York: Crossroad, pp. 1–14.

Segovia, F. F. (2000), 'Deconstruction' in Fabella, Virginia and Sugirtharajah, R. S. (eds), *Dictionary of Third World Theologies*, Maryknoll NY: Orbis.

Segundo, J. L. (1976), *The Liberation of Theology*, trans. J. Drury, Maryknoll NY: Orbis Books.

Smith, K. (1999) *Dogma*, View Askew Productions.

Soulen, R. N. and Soulen, R. K. (2001) *Handbook of Biblical Criticism*, third edition, Louisville and London: Westminster John Knox.

Spencer, F. S. (2003) *What Did Jesus Do? Gospel Profiles of Jesus' Personal Conduct*, Harrisburg PA: Trinity Press International.

Stackhouse Jr, J. G. (2004) 'Evangelicals and the Bible Yesterday, Today and Tomorrow' in R. M. Fowler, E. Blumhofer and F. F. Segovia (eds) (2004) *New Paradigms for Bible Study: The Bible in the Third Millennium*, New York: T and T Clark, pp. 185–206.

Stone, K. (2002) 'What Happens When "Gays Read the Bible"?' in *The Many Voices of the Bible*, Concilium 2002/1, London: SCM Press, pp. 77–85.

Sugirtharajah, R. S. (1995) 'Afterword: Culture Texts and Margins: A Hermeneutical Odyssey' in R. S. Sugirtharajah (ed.) *Voices from the Margins: Interpreting the Bible in the third world*, London: SPCK, pp. 457–75.

Sugirtharajah, R. S. (ed.) (1999) *Vernacular Hermeneutics*, Sheffield: Sheffield Academic Press.

Sugirtharajah, R. S. (2001) *The Bible and the Third World: Precolonial, colonial and postcolonial encounters*, Cambridge: Cambridge University Press.

Sugirtharajah, R. S. (2002) *Postcolonial Criticism and Biblical Interpretation*, Oxford: Oxford University Press.

Sugirtharajah, R. S. (2003) *Postcolonial Reconfigurations*, London: SCM Press.

Tamez, E. (2002) 'Reading the Bible Under a Sky Without Stars' in W. Dietrich and U. Luz (eds), *The Bible in a World Context: An experiment in cultural hermeneutics*, Grand Rapids and Cambridge: Eerdmans.

The Methodist Church (2004) *What is a Deacon?* London: The Methodist Church.

Theissen, G. (1987) *Psychological Aspects of Pauline Theology*, Edinburgh: T and T Clark.

Thurman, H. (1949) *Jesus and the Disinherited,* Nashville: Abingdon Press.

Tiffany, F. C. and Ringe, S. H. (1996) *Biblical Interpretation: A road map*, Nashville: Abingdon Press.

Tisdale, L. T. (1997) *Preaching as Local Theology and Folk Art*, Minneapolis: Fortress.

Toop, D. (1984, 1991, 2000) *Rap Attack African Rap to Global Hip Hop,* London: Serpent's Tail.

Trible, P. (1984) *Texts of Terror: Literary-Feminist Readings of Biblical Narratives*, Philadelphia: Fortress Press.

Trustees for Methodist Church Purposes (1999) *The Methodist Worship Book,* Peterborough: Methodist Publishing House.

Tutu, D. (1994) *The Rainbow People of God*, London: Doubleday.

Van der Woude, A. S. (1986) *The World of the Bible*, Grand Rapids: Eerdmans.

Walker, A. (1983, 2001) *The Color Purple*, London: The Woman's Press.

Warrior, R. A. (1995) 'A Native American Perspective: Canaanites, Cowboys and Indians' in *Voices from the Margins*, ed. R. S. Sugirtharajah, second edition, Maryknoll NY: Orbis, pp. 287–95.

Weber, H-R. (1995) *The Book that Reads Me*, Geneva: World Council of Churches.

Weems, R. J. (2003) 'Re-Reading for Liberation: African-American Women and the Bible' in S. Schroer and S. Bietenhard (eds) *Feminist Interpretation of the Bible and the Hermeneutic of Liberation*, London: Sheffield Academic Press, pp. 19–32.

West, G. O. (1999) 'Local is Lekker, but Ubuntu is Best: Indigenous Reading Resources from a South African Perspective' in Sugirtharajah, R. S. (ed.) *Vernacular Hermeneutics*, Sheffield: Sheffield Academic Press.

West, G. O. (2003) 'Reading the Bible in the Light of HIV/AIDS in South Africa' *The Ecumenical Review* 55(4): 335–44.

Wheeler, S. E. (1995) *Wealth as Peril and Obligation: The New Testament on possessions*, Grand Rapids MI: William B. Eerdmans Publishing Company.

Wink, W. (1992) *Engaging the Powers: Discernment and resistance in a world of domination*, Minneapolis: Fortress Press.

Wonneberger, R. (1990) *Understanding the BHS: A manual for users of Biblica Hebraica Stuttgartensia*, second edition Subsidia Biblica 8. Rome: Biblical Institute Press.

World Council of Churches Faith and Order (1998) *A Treasure in Earthen Vessels: An instrument for an ecumenical reflection on hermeneutics*, Geneva: World Council of Churches.

Wren, B. (1989) *What Language Shall I Borrow? God-talk in worship: a male response to feminist theology*, New York: Crossroad.

Wurthwein, E. (1994) *The Text of the Old Testament: An introduction to the Biblia Hebraica*, revised edition, Grand Rapids: Eerdmans.

Yorke, G. (2004) 'Bible Translation in Anglophone Africa and her Diaspora: A postcolonial agenda' in *Black Theology: An international journal*, vol. 2 (2): 153–66.

Index of Subjects

Index of Names

Index of Biblical References